ANSWERING GOD'S CALL

AND HAVING ONE'S LIFE TRANSFORMED

THADDEUS DOYLE C.C.

Published By

First published in Ireland in 1999 by Fr. Thaddeus Doyle, whose address from September 2002 is The House of Mission, Shillelagh, Arklow, Co. Wicklow, Ireland.

(Until September 2002, Fr. Doyle's main address is St. Kevin's, Tinahely, Arklow, Co. Wicklow.

First Print 5,000 copies 1999; 2nd print 5,000 copies in 2001

© Copyright 1999 Thaddeus Doyle C.C.

Thaddeus Doyle C.C. asserts the moral right to be identified as the author of this work.

ISBN 0 9536330 0 4

Sincere thanks

To those who helped with this book, and to all who have made this book possible by helping me on life's path.

Scripture References

Scripture quotations are from the R.S.V., Catholic Edition, 1966, Thomas Nelson and sons Ltd., copyright, except where otherwise indicated. Scripture quotations from the Good News Bible, British usage edition, 1976, published by The Bible Societies/ Harper Collins Publishers Ltd., copyright American Bible Society, 1966, 1971, 1976, 1982 are denoted GN. Used with permission.

Cover photo

The sun rises over Medjugorje, a powerful symbol of how the Risen Christ can penetrate our lives with His light and with the heat of His love - and also a little reminder of all the early mornings that went into writing this book.

To Get Fr. Doyle's Publications By Post

For details on how to obtain this book and other works by Fr. Thaddeus Doyle, please turn to pages 3 - 4

(For address, see top of this page)

Remembering Mother

On January 19th, 1999, my mother died, aged 92. For many priests, the loss of their second parent triggers sadness, even depression. But for me, it too was a time of joy, even if there were a few tears as I looked on her loving face for the last time. I feel deeply privileged to have had such a wonderful mother and to have had her so long. She was a person of prayer and faith, so I know where she has gone, and because I know that she is with Jesus, I know that she is now there for me all the time.

I am however blessed to have three wonderful brothers and a wonderful sister, together with their families.

"Answering God's Call"

By post, incl. P&P , direct from Fr. T. Doyle,(see address on page 2), 2001 prices.

Ireland & N. Ireland: 1 copy 6.50 euros; 5 or more copies 5.00 euros each; 10 or more 4.50 euros each.

Great Britain, (economy rate), 1 copy £5.00; 6 or more £4.00 each; 12 or more £3.50 each.

Europe: surface, 1 or more 6.50 euros each; 6 or more 5.00 euros each.

Rest of World, surface, 1 or more 8.00 euros; 5 or more 6.50 euros each.

(U.S. Canadian or Australian dollars also acceptable.)

Special Offer By Post

Confined to Ireland and G.B. (2001 prices)

I copy each of, "Answering God's Call", "A Shower of Blessings", "The Miracle Rosary", "But I Get Nothing Out Of Mass" and "God Has A Plan For You" for just 10 euros including post. (£7.50 sterling).

A recent back issue of "The Curate's Diary" just 80 cents extra. (£0.50 sterling).

After 2001, allow a little extra for increased postal costs.

For the Rest of the World (Surface)
Add 2.50 euros (£2) for extra postage costs.

Other publications by Fr. T. Doyle

The Curate's Diary

The Christian monthly magazine written especially for the ordinary person - simple short gripping articles, aimed at helping the reader come to a living faith in the power of Jesus to enter and transform lives.

Price 50 Euro Cent., By post, 12 monthly copies for 10 euros; G.B. Sterling £7.50; Airmail elsewhere £12.50   (2002 prices)

A Shower of Blessings

Around 1988, I developed my own way of praying that helped me to become open to personal healing and to God's love through prayer. After 10 years using it each day myself, in 1998 I had it printed in booklet form, calling it "A Shower of Blessings - Becoming open to God's transforming power through daily prayer." 60,000 copies sold..

Ireland & G.B: 1 copy, 1 euro; 2 or more copies 80 cents each; 10 or more copies 65 cents each; 65 or more (Ireland only) 50 cents each
Sterling 1 copy 75p; 2 or 3 copies 65p each; 4 or more copies 60p each; 10 or more 50p each.

"But I Get Nothing Out Of Mass"

An 80 page booklet that has brought the Mass alive for thousands, and resulted in many coming back to Mass.

Ireland and G.B: By post:- 1 copy 2 euros; 2 or more copies 1.75 euros each; 8 for 13 euros; 25 or more 1.30 euros each
Sterling:- 1 copy £1.60; 4 for £5.00; 25 or more £1.00

"God Has A Plan For You"

A special book to help you to become open to the special plan God has for your life.. To make it simple and interesting, I have shared stories from my own life and the lives of friends, and then drawn lessons from them. Same size and price as "But I Get Nothing Out ot Mass."

The Miracle Rosary

A way of praying the Rosary for those who find concentration difficult.
Ireland and G.B.; By Post, 1 copy 65 cents; 2 copies 1 euro; 5 copies 2 euros; 12 copies 4 euros; 24 copies 6.50 euros. (2002 prices)
Sterling:- 1 copy 50p; 12 copies £3.00; 24 copies £5.00

Please Note

These prices ONLY apply to direct purchases from Fr. T. Doyle.
For the address, see page 2

CONTENTS

The five o'clock book

For several years I felt called to write this book, but, having many other commitments, I kept putting it off. But every time I heard of a priest leaving or of a priest having problems, I felt convicted, felt that I had let him down. This sense of call was really hitting me. But how could I possibly find time to write such a book? Was I not overstretched already? Then one day I spoke very directly to Jesus, "If You want me to write this book, then you must make it possible for me to find the time."

That evening I attended a function. Another priest started to share with me about the time he wrote a parish history, and how, to make the time, he started getting up at 5.00am and working on it until morning Mass. I got the message! If he was prepared to arise at 5.00am for the sake of a parish history, should I not be prepared to do so for something that could possibly help people spiritually. Since then, this book has had for me a sort of subtitle, "The 5.00 o'clock book".

Quite often when I had material ready for working on or ideas forming in my mind, I awoke at exactly 5.00am - including this morning. Other mornings I felt a bit lazy, deciding that I needed the extra sleep, that my poor eyes would end up going all watery. Guess what! I started getting nuisance phone calls! Guess the time I started getting them at!! Between 5.10am and 5.30am on mornings that I had decided to sleep on! The Father would never prompt someone to make a nuisance phone call. However He does work all things for the good for those who love Him, and in His great love for us, He can take satan's tricks and use them for His purposes.

Again I got the message, that the Father wished me to put every effort into getting this book finished. Strangely, for me, I am not finding myself tired after all the early mornings.

1

Rescued by Jesus

I grew up in a loving home and went to a really good Primary School. I have hardly a negative memory from my first thirteen years. So a good foundation was laid. But, back then, if a country boy was to get secondary education, the only real option was boarding school. So at the age of 13, I went to St. Peter's College. For the first three weeks it was exciting, a real adventure. I admit that I was both hyperactive and somewhat restless in class.

This wasn't helped by the fact that I was unaware that I faced an entrance exam on arrival, and not having a good long distance memory, I did badly and ended up in the 'B' grade for the first three months. As a result I wasn't being mentally challenged, found some of the classes rather boring, and reacted by being restless. This may help explain, but it does not excuse, what happened next.

I got blamed for something which I didn't do and got a very severe beating for it. It was very strange really. The teacher actually caught two others in the act of a bit of harmless mick-acting at the back of the classroom, but then turned to me, and by some peculiar logic which I have never quite figured out, decided that if they were at it, I must have been behind it. I wasn't!

They got a light punishment, but I got a very severe one - I lost count of the high number of slaps. I was now angry with the two who had been involved in the mick-acting, because, when they saw that the teacher was blaming me, they agreed that I was behind it even though I wasn't involved at all. I immediately got into an argument with them. The teacher came back down, lost the run of himself and literally beat me around the room. It was a very severe beating, but no matter how much he beat me, I still insisted on my innocence. He then threatened to have me expelled. For me, it was a frightening threat:- the end of my secondary schooling after just three weeks and the disgrace it would involve.

For a thirteen year old who had always experienced fair play, and seldom seen corporal punishment and then only in real moderation, the whole thing was a frightening and bewildering experience. Worse was to follow. The two students responsible for this incident became members of a gang of bullies that caused immense hurt to many students. I was now in conflict with them, and, as a result, became their number one victim.

I suffered much at their hands especially over the next two years. Not merely did I suffer directly, but also I lived in a continuous state of fear. During my second year in particular, the situation was effectively out of control not just during recreation time, but also in both the classroom and the refectory. The bullies even controlled who got food at our table and how much or how little each person got - if any. There was a Leaving Cert student supposedly in charge, but so long as he got something himself, he said nothing. Indeed, sometimes, even he was rationed.

The same teacher was still running amok, though action was eventually taken. I won't go into details as I do not wish to cause either hurt or speculation and anyway I have long since forgiven the person responsible. One cannot forgive and keep rattling off all the details. It is important that one lets go of the past.

At the time, though I was an innocent victim, I took all the blame and shame upon myself. Deep down I really came to believe that it was I who had the problem. I was very angry with and bitter towards those who caused the hurt, but deep down it was myself I blamed.

It destroyed me from within; destroyed my sense of self-worth; destroyed my ability to concentrate; left me feeling deeply inadequate, different, and very isolated; not to speak of the effects of living in ongoing fear. I ended up a very broken person.

Thankfully, apart from one attempt by one of the bullies which I successfully resisted, I never suffered any form of sex abuse. However, when a teenager is deeply hurt, it affects the entire person, including one's sexuality. When one is both deeply hurt and deeply lonely, one turns in on oneself and begins to fantasise.

Yet I also desired to be a priest, to serve God, to preach the Gospel. Believing that everyone could see the inner turmoil I was going through, that people could know by looking at me, it came as a surprise when my application for the priesthood was accepted. Thankfully I was sent to St. Patrick's College, Maynooth, which gave me the chance of a new beginning. There was a great atmosphere there and the nobleness of my fellow seminarians absolutely amazed me. There was just one problem:- I had brought myself with me! The years of living in the valley of darkness had taken its toll and left many problems and compulsions.

I felt a complete fraud; felt that if the others knew the hidden me that I would be rejected. I was also full of anger and crippled by feelings of being inferior, of being different. I really gave it a big big try. But after five years I could go no further. I was desolate, even dangerously desolate. I just wanted to be no more. There were times when I was close to suicide. The one thing that saved me during this time of great darkness, was that I didn't wish to bring hurt to my family. I knew that they would be devastated if I ended my own life. That thought alone kept me going.

I was then so desolate that I could not visualise how I could be happy anywhere; not even in heaven. Yes, even heaven seemed a terribly desolate place and worse still, a desolate place that would just go on and on for ever.

In the Gospels I read Jesus' claim to be the 'Bread of Life'. I cried out to Him, 'If you really are the Bread of Life why am I experiencing such inner emptiness?'

That for me was a burning question; either He was who He claimed to be or there was something terribly wrong with the whole thing. He said that He was the Bread of Life, yet I had prayed daily, gone to Mass daily and there I was full of emptiness. There was a contradiction in all this. I had cried out but got no answer. I felt that I could no longer continue going for the priesthood, and so I told both my family and the appropriate authorities that I was quitting, and started serious job hunting.

— Then another student handed me a copy of "The Cross and the Switchblade' which describes how David Wilkerson had felt called by God to travel to New York and to start ministering to the street gangs. He had nothing bar the Gospels and the power of the Holy Spirit to bring to them, yet some of the toughest of the gang leaders had their whole lives transformed. They were taken from the streets, from the brutal violence, the robberies, the drug addiction, the promiscuity and given a whole new life.

It was like reading the Acts of the Apostles all over again - only now it was taking place today. My whole being was gripped with faith as I read that book. I knew that there was a power that could transform my life; that all I needed was to get to where people were walking and ministering in that power and I would be transformed.

I had never travelled abroad, indeed my insecurity made travel an ordeal, but I was determined that I was going to get to New York, to get to where the power of the Gospel to transform lives was being preached. Everything within me said that this was the answer. About a week or so later, Benny McHale, now Fr. Benny, a priest in the Tuam diocese, invited me to a Prayer Meeting in Maynooth. I thought it was marvellous:- those taking part seemed to be really experiencing Jesus as the Bread of Life, walking in a living relationship with Jesus.

Needless to say, given the interior crisis I was then undergoing, many things had become spiritually dry, spiritually empty for me. Even the Mass had lost its meaning, had lost its appeal, become empty. There appeared so much joy by comparison at the Prayer Meeting. The members had something that I so badly needed.

A few days later, I was walking down the corridor in Maynooth, when I met Benny, accompanied by Kevin Lanigan, later Fr. Kevin, a priest in Cork who died suddenly some years back. They were on their way to a big Prayer Meeting in Eustace Street in Dublin and had one seat left in the minibus - if I was interested. I didn't have to ask the Lord whether He wanted me to go!!!

Arriving in Eustace Street I was amazed by the crowds and took it for granted that everybody present had come into this mighty power. Some of their ways of praying, hand clapping, hands in the air, tongues etc., didn't come natural to me. But I didn't care. I really wanted what was behind it all, the power of the Holy Spirit.

There was an evangelist or minister from Belfast there that night. I believe he was a Presbyterian. I didn't get his name - something that is now a matter of deep regret to me. If I remember rightly, he showed a video of people who had been healed through his ministry. After the meeting I had the opportunity to be prayed with by him. I just mentioned my inner loneliness and he prayed, placing his hands on my head. Nothing happened while he was praying over me. In fact, I remember feeling a sense of disappointment.

Then some 15 to 30 seconds after I moved away from him, it started. Where deep within my chest I had previously experienced the centre of the great inner emptiness, inner vacuum, I now felt a bubbling heat beginning to rise; bubbling and swirling and filling out, like clouds billowing in the sky.

The Prayer Meeting had centred very much on the Holy Spirit. Having read 'The Cross and the Switchblade' I had believed that it would be the Holy Spirit that would transform me. Yet, as I experienced the bubbling, billowing sensations of heat moving within me as a living force, I also experienced a great conviction that it was the Risen Jesus who was present to me. I neither understood nor analysed it then. I just knew that I was feeling heat where previously I had experienced the emptiness, and somehow I knew I was being touched by Jesus.

The heat continued all the way back to Maynooth. I went to sleep with it that night. I woke up with it the next morning and went right through the day with it, and so indeed for several days, I now cannot remember how many. I do remember that about 10 days to two weeks later, I experienced a sense of panic for about 5 minutes. I suddenly realised that the heat was gone, but even as I panicked, I realised that there was something equally valuable in its place, a sense of calm and the continued and ongoing sense of the presence of Jesus.

Meanwhile I was telling my friends something of what had happened - though I found sharing very difficult. Some warned of emotional experiences, of the danger of coming down off the high, off cloud nine as they called it, and of being worse off than ever when I hit the ground. That was 27 years ago. Praise God, I still haven't hit the ground. Indeed while the heat has gone, the totality of the experience has never left me and indeed, especially in the last 12 years, has grown stronger and stronger and stronger. In an inner but yet very definite way, I have met the Risen Jesus. Jesus said,

"Whoever believes in Me, streams of life-giving water will pour out from His heart" John 7:37 (GN).

"Whoever drinks the water that I will give Him will never be thirsty again. The water that I will give him will become in him a spring of water welling up to eternal life." John 4:14, (GN)

That is what I experienced and that is what I am continuing to experience, now more than ever. Jesus has given me this spring of life-giving water and it is now indeed becoming a stream. My experience of it continues to grow.

Some people can testify that when Jesus came upon them, their every problem was removed, that they were cleansed of whatever bad habits they had built up in their hours of darkness and that all the hurt and anger was taken away. It was the total opposite with me. I experienced the power of the Risen Christ. Where previously there had been an ongoing sensation of inner emptiness, there was now an ongoing sensation of the presence and love of Jesus. But I was left to face every other compulsion, every other problem, every other area of difficulty that had built up in my life over the years.

I was still very far from being ready to even consider forgiving the people who had hurt me. I was carrying all the anger and bitterness and hadn't even begun to realise that, not merely was this contrary to the teaching of Jesus, but that it would delay my inner healing, and spill over in all sorts of ways in my life.

It was in October 1972 that Jesus touched my life. As a result I recommitted myself to going for the priesthood. But it still was by no means all plain sailing. I suffered deep feelings of inferiority, intense shyness, was full of anger, and despite Jesus having filled the emptiness, I still experienced some loneliness and even more so, a real fear of ending up lonely. I also found difficulties in coping sexually. Around this time, I had a very frank discussion with my spiritual director during which I outlined very candidly my difficulties with sex, and asked if he felt I should leave the Seminary. He acknowledged the extent of my difficulties, but said that he felt that I could make it.

Just one and a half years later, in June 1974, I was ordained, and begun my priestly ministry full of enthusiasm, but also still needing much healing. On the one hand I was working out of a very deep faith experience. On the other, there was still so much to be faced in my own life, so much healing required.

I can now see that for the first 13-14 years of my ministry, I was a divided person:- partly walking in the power of Jesus, yet still having to grapple with, face up to and even be delivered from all the knock-on effects of the years that I had spent in darkness, the damage that my whole person had suffered as a result of those traumatic teenage years. When there is both anger and insecurity within a person, it spills over. It leaves one sensitive, causes one to be judgemental, makes it difficult to cope with criticism or even differences of opinion. Small things are taken too seriously.

Not being able to cope, one lashes back and then divisions are formed. I must admit that I was guilty of this. May I express my apologies to those I hurt or let down during those years. The sad truth is that when one is hurt oneself and hasn't dealt with the hurt, one in turn hurts others. I was doing the best I was capable of, but I needed much inner healing. I still hadn't begun to forgive either the teacher or the bullies. Indeed, I must sadly confess that I would have rejoiced at their destruction. I totally avoided the teacher so that I wouldn't have to speak to him. My heart was still a long way from being open to the message of Jesus,

"If you do not forgive others, then your Father will not forgive the
wrongs you have done" Matthew 6:15, (GN).

It was several years before I came to see the importance of forgiveness, came to see that to be an authentic follower of Jesus one must forgive, came to see that it was necessary for my own inner healing. I now thank God for the day I found the grace to begin to forgive, and regret that that day didn't come sooner. It now greatly pleases me also that I never sought anything from those who brought the hurt into my life, never demanded retribution or justice, never even asked for an apology or an explanation.

I admit that there was a time when I felt very different about that and had it been in my power, I would have sought it. I am glad now that I never had that chance, that my forgiveness was real forgiveness and not based on anything they did.

Mind I am not saying that there isn't a time for confronting. When I used to have time for counselling, many abuse victims came to me. On some occasions I helped to prepare them to confront the abuser and supported them in so doing. There is also a time for challenging the system, for seeking to do one's bit to ensure that the mistakes of the past never happen again. I fully support those who seek to do that in a Christian way.

I also still think of others who suffered, including a couple of boys who suffered far more than I did at the hands of the teacher. I have no idea where they went or how they got on. I just pray that they were able to recover.

What happened in my own life brought me to my knees, led to great personal brokenness, led me to the verge of suicide, led to years of desolation, greatly affected my personality and my ministry for many years, but I give thanks to God for finding the grace to forgive without seeking to bring any form of hurt into the lives of those responsible.

I went through hell in my five years in St. Peter's. Arising from it, I went through great desolation for five of my seven years in Maynooth. For a further ten to twelve years after ordination, I was still struggling, still suffering the affects on my personality. Some effects remained much longer - forms of shyness, difficulties in mixing. Thank God, I feel that they too are now left behind.

I thank God for being able to let go of it all. I thank God for the gift of being able to forgive. I thank God for the wonderful ongoing healing that Jesus brings. I thank God that I am now beginning to glimpse the type of love that the Father has for us, unconditional love; love that does not require that the other person be nice in order for one to love; love that is prepared to love regardless of what a person has done even to oneself.

Strange to say, I also now thank God for all that happened to me. I now have a truly wonderful experience of Jesus as the bread of my life. I have learned so much through my own struggles, grown so much as I sought personal healing. My life is filled with an intense ongoing joy. One can never put back the clock. One can never be the same person that one would have been if these things had never happened. But one can, with the help of Jesus, become a better person. I believe that I am. Had these things not happened, you would not have this book to read.

My one and only regret is that, while I was still a divided person, I brought hurt into the lives of others. For that I sincerely apologise.

During the period when I was still struggling, celibacy and sexuality were also extremely difficult for me. It is not easy to write about such things. They are very personal. I do so for one reason only - to hold out hope to others. Jesus is interested in helping us in the sexual side of our being also. What is more, it is possible to experience sexual healing, to even be delivered from sexual compulsions. I can testify to that.

When one has suffered great hurt, it inevitably has a knock-on affect on one's sexuality. It is one of the consequences. In my case there was an extra factor. Sadly I had been led to believe that celibacy wasn't God's will and had been given the falsified version of its history which so many trot out to this day. This made it even harder still, much harder.

Then in 1987 I spent some days in a mobile at Ballinesker by the sea. While there, I had a brief spiritual experience.   While feeling a bit bored, I picked up a spiritual book by Jean Vanier, opened it and read, "Celibacy is a gift".   The words absolutely lit up. As the words "Celibacy is a gift" lit up, a flow of gentle energy seemed to pass through me, from my heart to my feet.

I can't rightly describe what happened. It was too quick, too gentle for words. Yet it was as if something was washed away, as if something literally left my body. I immediately felt a new sense of freedom, freedom from sexual compulsions.

That was 12 years ago. It was a further important turning point. I have found celibacy increasingly easy since then. I believe that the healing that started that day has been continued - especially each year at the Intercession For Priests. Three or four years ago, Sr. Briege McKenna gave me a little personal prophecy concerning victory in the sexual area of my life. I felt nothing either while she was praying with me or afterwards, but I haven't had what even could be termed a 'bad thought' since.

Around this time, I also discovered the truth about the rule of sexual continence in the early Church; that while married men were free to be ordained, that thereafter they were expected to renounce their marriage, to live as brother and sister with their wives. All the evidence indicates that this rule went right back to the time of the Apostles. Learning this was an eye opener.

Every time I now see falsified accounts of the history of celibacy I feel a sense of anger. It is tough enough to live celibacy when one knows that it is God's will, but when one is led to believe that it isn't God's will, it becomes a great burden.

Meanwhile I find it hard to find words to express the joy and happiness that is in my life. It is a truly wonderful ongoing experience. It all comes from my relationship with Jesus, the outpouring of the Holy Spirit and the love of the Father. I write this book in the hope that you too will become open to something of what God desires to do in your life, something of the blessings that could be yours.

2

From Death Wish To Unspeakable Joy

"You will weep and lament, but the world will rejoice; you will be
sorrowful, but your sorrow will turn into joy." John 16:20

When I was in despair, I had begun to realise that if Jesus was who He said He was, there had to be something missing in my experience of the faith. He claimed to be the Bread of Life. I had prayed hard, I had gone to Mass daily, I had expressed a willingness to serve Him, but yet I felt so empty that it ached. It didn't add up.

At the time it appeared that I was losing the faith. In a sense I was. The faith as I had known it was no longer able to answer my questions or fill my needs. There appeared to be a contradiction at the centre of it. In reality, God was preparing me for something far greater. I was being helped to realise that if Jesus was real, then there had to be more to the faith than I had been led to expect.

I now know that the very heart of the Gospel message is that Jesus is the Bread of Life. He desires to really come to live in us, to become our very best Friend. The Gospel is the Good News about how you and I can be transformed, about a wonderful experience of new life that is available to us, about how we can be set free from our compulsions, experience inner healing and be brought into a wonderful new experience of living.

"He who believes in me, as the scripture has said, 'Out of his heart
shall flow rivers of living water'" John 7:38.

Jesus promised the woman who had tried to satisfy her inner needs with many relationships,

"Whoever drinks of the water that I shall give him will never thirst
(again), the water that I shall give him will become in him a spring of
water welling up to eternal life" John 4:14.

↳   It is out of one's heart that the life giving waters shall flow. The centre of one's spirit is within one's chest.   When I was going through my time of great emptiness and desolation, it was within my chest that I felt the emptiness. At some of the really bad times, it was like as if there was a great bottomless hole within my chest. At other bad times, it was like as if there was a great vacuum within my chest sucking me in.

Today I also experience a lot within my chest, but it is an experience of great joy. So often within my chest there is the sensation of fullness; an experience of joy continuously welling up. There are times when I literally find myself gasping with joy. I know exactly what Jesus was speaking about when He used the image of the life giving water welling up within. I know because I have experienced!

The depth of joy I now experience is not something that I have come into over night. Far, far from it!! First I had a deep spiritual experience, a life transforming experience. But after that I had so much to face up to, so many elements of my 'old self' to deal with, so many tough choices to make. I am writing this 27 years after my initial experience, 27 years of choices and decision making, 27 years of seeking to grow in my relationship with Jesus and in my openness to the workings of the Holy Spirit.

Looking back I can see that the real growth in joy only truly began after I had both forgiven those who had hurt me and had been freed from my sexual compulsions. Prior to that I was a split person, part of me was experiencing the wonderful new life, yet another part was still in darkness. What I was experiencing in my spiritual centre was not yet flowing through the rest of my being.

I know what it is like to be a person of two halves; to have a deep personal relationship with Jesus and to desire to serve God on the one side, yet getting caught up in divisions, causing hurt and giving way to personal weakness on the other. I know because I have been there. May I once again express my sincerest apology to anyone I failed or into whose life I brought hurt during those years.

The most important first step had already taken place. I had a deep personal relationship with Jesus. He had become for me the Bread of Life. He had entered where previously there had been the terrible emptiness. The inner spiritual centre of my being had a Resident. It remained, however, for Him to truly become Lord of my life.

It also remained for my spirit to grow to its proper maturity, nor was it possible for this to happen while I was still split. A sinner can meet Jesus, have a deep personal encounter with Him, but tough choices will be necessary if there is to be real maturing, real growth in the spirit, real openness to the fruit of the Spirit.

But let us get back to basics. As well as a brain, each of us has a spiritual centre, what some call the inner room that has been made specially for Jesus and which only Jesus can fill. If this is not being filled by Jesus and his love, there will be great emptiness within. There are no substitutes, not even religion! One may be a religious person, one may say many prayers, but one still needs to experience Jesus in this personal way and one still needs to have one's life transformed. Without being touched by the love of God, one's spiritual centre remains thirsting, remains seeking.

It also remains at best underdeveloped, and possibly even undeveloped, because it only begins to develop and to grow as it begins to be filled by Jesus and His love. This is an important point though hard to put into words.

We have many important body parts. The most important is the spirit. Just like any other body part, it needs to be cared for, nourished, and used for the purposes for which it was created. A person who has been confined to bed for a prolonged period has to learn to walk all over again. Think how atrophied one's legs would be if one never used them. That is exactly what many people's spirits are like, atrophied, undeveloped, suffering from malnutrition.

Just as one's legs are for walking, one's spirit is for spiritual experience, for the entry of Jesus into one's life, for receiving the fruits of the Holy Spirit. Without Jesus plus spiritual nourishment and spiritual exercise, one's spirit becomes like a limp empty sack. Ask most people to tell you where the centre of their spirit is, and they won't even know what you are talking about.

27 5. 06. — Jesus spoke of the need to be baptised with the Holy Spirit. The original secular word, from which the word Baptism is derived, means to be flooded with and also to be dyed through and through with. When the early Christian writers spoke of being baptised into Jesus, this is what they had in mind; total penetration, being flooded with the living presence of Jesus, having one's inner spirit filled and one's entire personality dyed through and through by Him and with Him.

When Jesus spoke of being baptised in the Spirit, he was thinking not of a neat little ritual, but total penetration by the Holy Spirit. We read in Acts that they were all "filled with the Holy Spirit" Acts 2:4. Some believe that this type of experience was only for the early Church. This is totally wrong. It even contradicts Scripture. St. Peter makes clear that the promise is for all God's people of every time and place.

"The promise is to you and to your children and to all that are far off, every one whom the Lord our God calls to Him" Acts 2:39.

It is also contradicted by history. Early Church history shows that, for several hundred years, the Church expected that those who were baptised would live transformed lives. Current history shows that many are still experiencing the Baptism of the Spirit just like in the early Church. May I number myself amongst them. While writing this book, I made a decision to write of nothing that I had not personally experienced.

It is God's wish that every person be filled with the Holy Spirit. If you are not filled with the Holy Spirit, it is not God's fault. It may not be your fault either. But it is now up to you to do something about it. If you don't, then it will be your fault.

Once one begins to truly experience Jesus, once one's spirit is baptised, flooded, then great things begin to happen, great changes become possible, though one may still have many tough choices to make and much persevering to do.

But down the road, in my case well down the road, once one's spirit becomes strong, as well as experiencing great joy, one becomes filled with a great strength. The stronger one's spirit, the greater the capacity to take the events of life in one's stride. The Spirit-filled spirit is a very strong spirit, one that can truly face anything.

The apostles and early Christians spoke from personal experience. When they spoke of new life in Jesus, they did so, not because they had read about it in a book, but because that is what they were experiencing. They had discovered that when the Risen Jesus entered one's life, it led to a whole new experience of living, led to one being transformed. It really was 'new life'.

When they spoke of how Jesus took our 'old self' with Him to the Cross so that we could experience deliverance from bad habits, they were speaking of a reality that they had already discovered in their own lives. They had discovered that when the Risen Jesus entered one's life, real and profound changes became possible; that one could be set free from one's compulsions.

When they spoke of fruits of the Spirit, and gave a list of them, they spoke from personal experience. They had discovered that, when one opened one's spirit to the working of the Holy Spirit, one began to notice a real change coming from within. Hence St. Paul could say,

"The fruit of the Spirit is love, joy, peace, patience, kindness, goodness, faithfulness, gentleness, self-control" Galatians 5.22.

St. Paul had discovered this to be true in the school of personal experience. Again it is within one's chest, within one's spiritual centre, that one experiences the fruits of the spirit. They all have to do with what is referred to as the workings of the heart. The more one experiences Jesus and His love, the more one's spirit and one's spiritual capacity is developed, and hence the more open one becomes to the fruits:- love, joy, peace, etc. Their arrival and development in turn leads to an even further development of one's spirit.

29/5/06

A new capacity to love all people is the first fruit of the Spirit. Ongoing spiritual joy is the second. Today, 27 years after Jesus became the Bread of Life for me, 27 years of growth through trial and error, this joy is at the very centre of my being. I say that not to draw attention to myself, but to draw attention to what Jesus desires that you experience:- unspeakable joy.

To come into this joy, to grow in it, one must first experience Jesus as the Bread of Life, and then learn to live by His teaching. The Holy Spirit cannot enter where there is serious personal sin, cannot enter where there is selfishness. The Holy Spirit can only enter our lives to the extent to which we are prepared to open them to Jesus. This involves facing whatever needs to be faced, repenting of whatever needs to be repented.

If you are in a wrong relationship, do NOT expect to receive the fruits of the Spirit and do not expect to see great blessing until you have renounced the relationship. If there is great anger and bitterness in your life, again do not expect to experience the fruits of the Spirit or great answers to prayer until you at least desire to deal with the anger. The same applies to each of the seven deadly sins:- pride, covetousness, lust, anger, gluttony, envy and laziness.

In each case, may I stress that I am not suggesting that Jesus does not love you or that He cannot come into your life. He was in my life for many years before I got myself sorted out, but I was not experiencing the fruits of the Spirit nor was I seeing great blessing. Jesus desires your life to be filled with great joy, but I know what He meant when He said,

"If you keep the commandments, you will abide in my love, just as I have kept my Father's commandments and abide in his love. These things I have spoken to you, that my joy may be in you, and that your joy may be full." John 15:10-11

Jesus desires that we live joy filled lives. He desires that you too experience the joy and the energy that now fills so much of my life. But, before this can even begin to happen, you must begin to respond. You must learn what it is to abide in His love. And abiding in His love involves keeping the commandments.

31. 05. 06.

3

Becoming open to the New Life

Many think that the reason they find the New Testament dry or boring is because it was written 2,000 years ago. However the real reason is that it speaks of realities that they are not experiencing in their own lives. The New Testament tells us of a wonderful experience of new life that Jesus desires us to have, but if one is not experiencing that new life, worse still, if one doesn't even believe that such new life is possible, what it says just passes over one's head. However, once one begins to experience what the early Christians experienced; begins, that is, to experience the living and transforming power of Jesus, then the words of the New Testament spring to life.

I studied the Bible in Seminary, did a degree in it, yet, at that time, I too found it boring because I did not have personal experience of the new life of which it spoke. Then I experienced Jesus as the Bread of Life, and, bit by bit, the whole New Testament started to register. As I grew in my relationship with Jesus, the entire New Testament came to life.

It speaks of something truly powerful, of how our inner selves can literally be filled with Jesus, of how our lives can be transformed by Him, of how the Holy Spirit can really start to work in our lives once we have learned to walk with Jesus, of how Jesus invites us to a very real and truly fabulous experience of the Father and His love.

We are called to allow Jesus to so live in us, to allow his light and His love to so flow right through us that, not merely does He live in us, but we also live in Him.

"It is no longer I who live, but Christ who lives in me" Galatians 2:20.

We are called to be literally flooded with His presence. When I speak of being flooded with Jesus, of Him coming to live within one's spirit, within one's heart room, and then penetrating the rest of one's being with His light and His love, I speak of a lived reality. This is what I experience in my daily life.

I have been a slow learner. I have made many mistakes. Of myself, I can only think of my own sinfulness, my own unworthiness. Jesus has been very patient with me. Looking back, I can see that He was there helping me and protecting me even when I was a mixed-up teenager. Indeed I now deeply believe that on many occasions He protected me from the consequences of my own mistakes.

Patiently, amidst everything, Jesus has led me to a level of tremendous personal transformation. First He filled me with His love. Then, step by step, He has led me through a process of healing, deliverance, growth and transformation. It has been slow. It has been, at times, painful. It has required me to persevere; to hang in there even when I couldn't see progress. But slowly, gradually, Jesus has been penetrating the depths of my personality, the layers of my mind and heart.

Father desires that you experience this also. I do not hold out any quick fixes, nor soft options, but I do hold before you the most wonderful ongoing experience open to humankind:- to have Jesus become for you the Bread of Life, to have your life gradually transformed by Him, to come to experience Father's love, to become open to the fruits of the Holy Spirit and then to the power of the Holy Spirit.

The Sacraments

Recently I saw the account of an amazing rescue of a little two week old puppy. The little puppy had wandered from its nest, fallen down a five foot hole and then fallen through a crack into a sewer pipe. Then it was swept along by the effluent. Goodbye puppy! One would have thought. But no! People set out to rescue it. One person got the type of camera that can be fed down into a drain. It located the puppy several yards away out under the street.

Then they got in a digger and dug right down through the street, then cracked the sewer pipe open and lifted the puppy out. Had the operation to be paid for, it would have cost over £10,000. But it was all given free. The thought struck me - that's just like God's love, both incredible and free. Except for one detail:- the puppy was lifted out by the hair of the head, whereas God will never force us. He desires to rescue us, but we must co-operate.

Jesus gave us the sacraments as part of His rescue mission, as opportunities for transformation; opportunities for us to welcome Him into our lives, and to be transfigured through Him.

When I see the way the sacraments are presented today, it makes my blood boil! How we have tied the sacraments up into neat little rituals, even become obsessed with the externals of the ritual. The extent to which talks about Baptism, Confirmation and the Eucharist focus just on the ritual really saddens me. Imagine getting a lecture about a bar of chocolate and the entire talk centring on the wrapping paper. Imagine getting a lecture on a new motor car and the entire talk centring on the paint and decoration. Focusing primarily on the ritual is akin to focusing on the wrapping paper rather than on the actual chocolate, akin to focusing on the decor of a motor car rather than its capacity to get from A to B.

The decor of the car is very important, but unless the car can go, unless it is a bundle of dynamic energy, then the decor has very limited value. So too with the sacraments. They are meant to be vehicles of transformation, occasions of coming into an experience of the power and love of God. The outward signs of the sacraments are meant to correspond with what is happening within the person.

To truly be baptised isn't just to have water poured over one's head. The word 'baptise' means to be flooded with. The pouring of the water symbolises what Jesus desires to do within us, how He desires for His light and His love to so penetrate us, that they flood every area of our being. Until this begins to happen, one's sacramental Baptism hasn't been confirmed. There is a most important sense in which it has not been consummated.

I had been baptised, confirmed, and was receiving Holy
Communion regularly, indeed I was even studying for the
priesthood, but I was in a terrible state. Not merely was I not
being flooded with the love of Jesus, but I hadn't even experienced
Him as the Bread of Life. I had received all the sacraments, but I
had not yet come into the new life that Jesus desires that we receive
through these same sacraments.

It is very significant that Jesus sandwiched His instruction on
going out to baptise between the instruction to make disciples and
the instruction to teach them to observe all that He has commanded.
*"Go therefore and make disciples of all nations, baptising them in the
name of the Father and of the Son and of the Holy Spirit, teaching
them to observe all that I have commanded you" Matthew 28:19-20.*

There are three steps. First we are to make disciples, that is
bring them to Jesus, get them to make a decision for Jesus. Then
we are to baptise, that is we lead them into an experience of being
flooded with this new life. Then we are to teach them to observe
all that Jesus commanded so that they may grow in the new life.

Before we can be flooded with God's love a real change has to
take place:- we must turn to Jesus, become disciples, repent of our
selfishness, desire God's way. That doesn't come easy.

Humankind has a fear of the Gospel. The message of Jesus is
too radical. It demands change, demands inner transformation,
demands that we be willing to let go of our selfish ways, challenges
us to renounce our independent decision making, challenges us to
enter a relationship of incredible intimacy.

All this is very frightening. Is it any wonder that so many run a
mile, that even religious people want to settle for a safe comfortable
religion that can be satisfied by saying prayers? The history of
our Church is the history of a people who so often have kept the
outer forms of Christianity while denying its power. What St.
Paul prophesied has come true,
*"In the last days, ... men will be lovers of pleasure rather than lovers
of God, holding the form of religion but denying the power of it" 2
Timothy 3:1-5.*

5. 06 06

We desire to tame the message of Jesus, to still have the glamour of being Christians, but to turn it into a safe religion, a religion that is not too challenging, not too demanding; a religion where one can go through the motions, but not have to be transformed. How better to do that than to tie it up in a set of neat little rituals where nothing dramatic happens and no real change is expected.

This is not an attack upon the Sacraments, but upon the superficial way in which they are currently being understood and presented.   Jesus gave us the Sacraments as occasions of transformation, occasions when we could renounce self and come into a deeper experience of His life changing love. We, however, have turned them into safe, non-challenging little rituals.

The worst thing that ever happened in the Church was the way Baptism came to be understood after the widespread introduction of infant Baptism.   Mind I am not attacking infant Baptism itself. Twice, in the Acts of the Apostles, we see people being baptised together with their entire household. First there was Lydia and her household, Acts 16:15.   Then there is the truly remarkable story of the jailer in Acts 16:25-34. This is truly remarkable, not just because he was baptised with all his family, but because of the promise that Paul and Silas made him,

"Believe in the Lord Jesus, and you will be saved, and your household" Acts 16:31.

That is a most consoling promise. A parent who is truly converted can in some way bring about the salvation of his or her family. How appropriate it is, then, that parents claim that salvation for their children by having them baptised.

What I am challenging is the superficial way in which Baptism is now understood and accepted. The widespread introduction of infant Baptism made possible a situation where one could have the administration of a sacrament without any visible change being either expected or possible. How well that suits those who want a non-demanding religion, who want neat little rituals that effect no visible change. How totally and utterly removed that is from the challenging and transforming message of the Gospel, from the faith as lived and experienced in the early Church.

Jesus doesn't just tell us about God, doesn't just win for us forgiveness for our sins. He offers us 'New Life'. Not merely does he offer us this 'New Life', He confronts us with the need to live it.

"Unless a person is being born anew he cannot see the Kingdom of God" John 3:3.

We Catholics have largely turned a blind eye to this passage about being born again. It just hasn't been part of our vocabulary. We have paid the price for this neglect and are continuing to pay it. There is a connection between the scandals that our Church is currently facing and our blindness to John 3:3, the demand that one must be born again.   We have neither challenged people to rebirth nor held out to them the wonderful transformation that it can bring.   We have created and given legitimacy to the Church of the unconverted, the Church where rebirth is no longer expected or demanded.   Is it any wonder that we have problems? Is it any wonder that even our leaders have fallen so far short, have behaved in shameful ways?

If one has serious problems in one's own life, it is not possible to live by the teaching of Jesus without first having been transformed by the presence, love and power of Jesus. Jesus came with Good News, came preaching a Gospel of transformation and personal empowerment.   We have turned it into a message of powerless rituals.

Baptism is often described as a ritual through which new members are enrolled in the Church, and this ritual is further compared to rituals that other organisations perform on new members. Confirmation is called a rite of passage from childhood to adulthood. But was it to become a member of the Church that Jesus was Baptised? Or was the coming of the Holy Spirit upon Him a rite of passage from childhood to adulthood? Was it about going through a ritual to become a member of the Church that Jesus was speaking when He declared that one must be reborn of water and the Holy Spirit?   Was this the understanding of the primary function of Baptism that they had in the early Church?

Most certainly not!!   Jesus most certainly was not baptised to join an organisation. His Baptism had everything to do with His relationship to His Father and the outpouring of the Holy Spirit. At the occasion of His Baptism, the Holy Spirit came upon Him in a very special way, He had a deep experience of the love of the Father, and, arising from His Baptism, He went forth with the Good News, the Gospel message.

"When Jesus was baptised, he went up immediately from the water, and behold the heavens were opened and he saw the Spirit of God descending like a dove and alighting on him; and lo, a voice from heaven, saying, 'This is my beloved Son, with whom I am well pleased'" Mt. 3:16-17.

So it was for Jesus and so it should be for us:- the purpose of the sacraments is to bring us into a real encounter with Jesus, to enable us to face whatever needs facing in our own lives, and then to lead us into an experience of Father's love and into a new openness to the Holy Spirit. When this takes place, as a result of it, we become part of Christ's body, the Church.

The combined sacraments of Baptism-Confirmation are, indeed, meant to be a rite of passage, but this has nothing to do with becoming an adult. They are meant to be a rite of passage into the wonderful new life that Jesus desires us to experience. They are meant to be a rite of passage during which we face whatever needs facing in our lives, so that we can begin to live the transformed life, with Jesus as our best Friend, with a deep experience of Father's love and with a real outpouring of the Holy Spirit.

Infant Baptism is fine so long as there is a proper procedure for its confirmation. It is fine where the young person is taught to expect to be touched by God's love and then given an opportunity to make an adult 'Yes' to their Baptism. But where that doesn't happen, it creates a Church of the baptised unconverted. This, in itself, is an utter contradiction, a real nonsense, because Baptism requires conversion for its consummation.

In dealing with marriage break-up we have developed an elaborate system for establishing the validity of marriage. Unless certain important conditions are met, we consider the marriage null and void. It is totally right that similar, though not identical, principles be applied to Baptism-Confirmation.

There is as grave an injustice involved in our current system of infant Baptism, where there isn't an adequate follow-up, as there was with infant marriages. We consider people to be fully fledged Christians just because someone poured a drop of water on their heads and because as young school children they are marched forward for Holy Communion and Confirmation. Then we expect them to be able to live by Christian teaching - including agape self-giving love and indissoluble marriage.

One cannot become a Christian without a personal decision, nor is one's personal decision complete until it becomes an adult decision.   The sacrament is not completed until the child freely expresses this consent itself, and freely seeks to enter into the fullness of baptismal living.

A further injustice, in the current system of infant Baptism, is that the person is denied the opportunity to either prepare for this wonderful sacrament or else to come into the blessings later. They are denied the opportunity to seek the promised outpouring and denied the opportunity to use it as an occasion of personal transformation.   This injustice could be removed by providing proper opportunities for a realistic renewal of Baptism, and by stressing the need of these for the consummation of one's Baptism.

In the early Church, Holy Saturday was a vigil of expectation. Those being baptised really expected the Holy Spirit to come upon them, really expected to live transformed lives thereafter. Those already baptised expected to grow in what they had already received, to come more fully into it.

How we need to rediscover the riches of the early church! How we need to put rebirth and personal transformation not just back on the agenda, but at the very centre of it!   How we need to ensure that the Sacraments are not treated as mere rituals, but as occasions for seeking real union with Jesus, real personal transformation, the real outpouring of the Holy Spirit, and a real experience of Father's love.

7. 06:06.-

4

The Need for Rebirth

My greatest joy springs from my relationship with Jesus and the transformation that He has brought in my life. As I have grown spiritually, the level of joy in my life has grown. I now truly live a joy-filled life. My greatest sorrow comes from the fact that Jesus, as I know Him, and inner transformation, as I have experienced it, are not being preached today as they should be.

I owe everything to Jesus. First I experienced Him as the Bread of Life. Then there was a slow process in which I eventually faced what needed to be faced in my life, and I became open to Jesus' power to transform from within. As a result, I became more open to the Holy Spirit. Now there is tremendous joy. I can truly say that my life is filled with great joy, ongoing joy.

Father desires this rebirth, this ongoing transformation and this joy for everybody. Yet, not merely are the majority not experiencing it, but the message of personal transformation, of the possibility of Jesus entering one's life, of Jesus truly becoming the Bread of Life, of one learning to surrender one's life to Him, of real rebirth is not even been preached.

The Church is paying a terrible price for this failure. The scandals are but one of many symptoms of a Church that hasn't led its members into rebirth. Add in the number dropping from Mass, the number abandoning prayer, the number leaving the Church, the number joining sects, the lack of missionary spirit, the fall off in vocations, the number of abortions, the breakdown in marriage. Again and again we are faced with the symptoms of how we have allowed our Church to become the Church of the unconverted rather than the Church that leads people into a real heart relationship with Jesus, to a change that comes from within, to rebirth and inner transformation.

Instead of the modern Nicodemus being challenged to be reborn, he is being told, at best, how to become a more religious person; or at worst, that he doesn't have to be so religious, since God loves him anyway. Nicodemus, as a leading Pharisee, was a very religious man. He had a strong belief in God. He prayed several times a day. He was scrupulous in keeping the commandments. To us, he had every qualification needed for being a good Christian. We would consider him suitable to be a priest or even to be a bishop. Jesus saw things very differently; told him that he must be reborn; that is, that he needed to be transformed from within, a rebirth that would begin with the heart.

"Unless one is born anew, he cannot see the Kingdom of God"
John 3:3.
"Unless one is born again of water and the Spirit, he cannot see the kingdom of God" John 3:5.

Believing in God isn't enough. Being loyal to prayer isn't enough. Practising virtue isn't enough. Something very radical is still required, so radical that Jesus described it in terms of being born again. We need to open our hearts to Jesus, to invite Him into our lives, and to seek to become open to what He has won for us and to what He desires to do within us. Instead of doing things for God, we need to become open to what God desires to do in us. Instead of working out of our own power and strength, we need to seek to become open to God's power, and the strength that comes from learning to depend on Jesus. After that, we need to seek total transformation by allowing Jesus to transform us from within.

Rebirth is a process. Emphasise the word 'process'. One's rebirth is not complete while there is any area of one's life that is not under the Lordship of Jesus. One's rebirth is not complete if one is still unforgiving. One's rebirth is not complete if one has serious sexual compulsions, or pride, or covetousness, or a need to prove oneself, or a drink problem or is dishonest or gossips or tells lies.

One may have a deep experience of Jesus' presence and His love, but until He is Lord of every area of one's life, one's rebirth is not complete. Jesus doesn't just desire to come into one's life, He desires to transform it. First He comes to live in us. Then we should seek to become so open to Him, that His light will shine in every area of our mind and heart. This involves opening all our memories to Him, surrendering all our attitudes to Him for transformation, and learning to walk through each day with our hand in His hand. It involves, above all, being willing to enter into a deep personal union with Him, having one's inner spirit filled with His love and His presence. Then, if we are willing, He enables us to face our every tendency towards wrongdoing.

We were born with a tendency towards wrongdoing. None of us had to learn how to do wrong. The instinct was already there. *"Sin came into the world through one man and death through sin, and so death spread to all men because all men sinned" Rom 5:12.*

When Joey was just beginning to walk, he got a little baby sister. Instead of being delighted, he was jealous. Several times he was caught pulling her ear or her hair. Nobody had to tell him how to hurt her. It just came naturally to him.

When we act out our tendency towards wrongdoing, the tendency grows and invades our attitudes and thoughts. But Jesus is willing to enable us to be transformed; gradually enabling us to face all the things that need to be faced. His love and his light can touch every area of our being, can go right back with us in time, freeing us from the wrong tendencies that we have built up, then eventually reaching right down to the roots of our wrong responses until His light and love begins to shine upon the original instinct for wrongdoing within us . That is what being born again means. We were born with a tendency towards sin. Now, by the grace of God, we can be reborn with that tendency increasingly broken.

The Church Calendar and Rebirth

In the early Church, they had great expectations of Baptism. It was the sacrament through which they expected their lives to be transformed. They were led to really expect Jesus to touch their lives, to really expect the Holy Spirit to come upon them and to really expect a realisation of how deeply Father loved them. They were further both led to expect, and challenged to live, transformed

lives.   The great disadvantage of infant Baptism is that all this
gets lost.   This would not, however, be such a problem if proper
use was made of the Liturgical Calendar to bring people to a proper
appreciation of their Baptism and to enable them to renew it.

The Church calendar has changed very little since the early
Church. It was formed by people who had a powerful relationship
with Jesus, people who were living transformed lives.   Hence,
just as the New Testament comes to life when one begins to
experience the realities it speaks of, so too does the Church calendar.
Again and again, for those who have eyes to see, ears to hear, the
Church calendar speaks of the wonderful new life that is available
to us and provides opportunities for us to grow in that new life.

Feast of Baptism of Jesus

In the early Church, Jesus' baptism was seen as the model and
paradigm of all baptism. Of course, unlike us, Jesus did not have
personal sin to repent of, yet at His baptism, as at Calvary, He took
our sins upon Himself. Then coming up from the water, He received
the outpouring of the Holy Spirit, and heard Father's voice
declaring, "This is my beloved son with whom I am well pleased"
Mt. 3:17. Then, after His Baptism, He entered on a whole new
life. The renewal of one's Baptism, opening oneself to the Holy
Spirit, coming into a special experience of Father's love should be
at the heart of the celebration of the Feast of Jesus' Baptism.   Yet
all this is, so often, totally ignored.

Easter - A Time For Rebirth

In the 'Constitution on the Sacred Liturgy', Vatican Two says,
"The Lenten season has a twofold character: 1) it recalls baptism or
prepares for it;   2) it stresses a penitential spirit."
"Wider use is to be made of the baptismal features proper to the
Lenten liturgy; some elements which belonged to a now-lapsed
tradition may be opportunely restored."
When Vatican 11 speaks of the twofold character of Lent, namely
recalling Baptism and stressing a penitential spirit, it is speaking
of two realities that go hand in hand; saying 'No' to self in order to
say 'Yes' to God; dying to self so as to rise to new life.

So many people generously make sacrifices and give up things for Lent. Our children give wonderful example in this. But how often are they told the primary purpose of making sacrifices, that it is to help one to become open to Jesus, to personal transformation, to the working of the Holy Spirit?

Then there is the Easter Vigil on Holy Saturday night. In the early Church, at the Easter Vigil, they had the blessing of the Baptismal Water followed by the baptisms. We have the blessing of the Easter Water, the sprinkling with it and the renewal of baptismal promises. In other words, a ceremony of Renewal of Baptism is already built into the Holy Saturday ceremonies.

In the early church, Lent was the period of the final stage of preparation for Baptism. For us, it should be a time of preparation for the Renewal of Baptism followed by the actual renewal on Holy Saturday. If we only began to do this, how much deeper would be people's understanding of the meaning and significance of their Baptism, how much more open might they become to Jesus and to personal rebirth, personal transformation!

Then there are the 50 days to Pentecost, 50 days of celebrating Easter, 50 days for preparing to become open to the Holy Spirit. However it is rare for one to have a Pentecost experience before one has an Easter experience. If we don't lead our people into the Easter experience of rebirth in Jesus, they cannot become open to Pentecost, to the outpouring of the Holy Spirit.

First one needs to come into a real relationship with Jesus. Then one needs to become open to inner transformation. Only then is one open to the outpouring of the Holy Spirit and to a deep experience of the fruit of the Spirit.

Until we have experienced Easter, until Jesus is in residence, until there is real transformation, there can be no real Pentecost, no outpouring of the Holy Spirit.

Growth In The Spirit

There cannot be real growth until we seek rebirth. Unless there is a process of change that springs from the heart and that leaves us desiring to experience real conversion, a real change in our attitudes, there will not be growth. Not merely will there not be growth, but there will be boredom. God's love can only be poured into our hearts once we become open to change from within, once we desire to take on the mind and attitudes of Christ. If you desire to grow, if you desire to come into the joy, start to face what needs to be faced in your thoughts and attitudes. Open yourself to rebirth and real inner transformation.

Growth requires tough decisions. It requires one to be single-minded about seeking it. Think of the many industrialists who regularly get up at 5.00am for the sake of their businesses! If we brought half the same zeal and commitment to our search for growth in Jesus, we would soon have the Church of the transfigured.

Growth requires ongoing personal decisions concerning how we order our lives, concerning what we do, where we go, what we eat, when we go to bed, when we get up, what we watch, what we read, etc. Above all, it requires us to face anything that is selfish or unloving in our attitudes and actions.

For me as a priest, ongoing growth is absolutely vital. I am dependent on Jesus to fill my life, to bring me fulfilment and inner strength, to even provide the nourishment that the married person draws from their marriage. Either I really experience Jesus as the Bread of Life or I become dysfunctional, stunted.

The Mass is the sacrament of Christian growth. What a truly great privilege it is to be able, each day, to join with Jesus in His offering of Himself to Father, to be able to join in spirit in the Last Supper, to be able to be united with Our Lady and St. John at the foot of the cross, to be able to welcome the Risen Jesus to dwell within us. Even thinking about celebrating Mass fills me with a sense of anticipation.

It is the most challenging and transforming experience open to a person:- to be united with Jesus' self-offering, His total offering of self, His conscious giving of Himself to His Father for us; to be immersed into Jesus Himself; to have Him, the Risen Jesus come live within us; to desire to be flooded with His love, to desire to have His living presence touch every area of one's being, and to unite with Him in calling down Father's blessing on one's parish.

5

When Celibacy is experienced as a Burden

When I was ordained, I saw celibacy as a rule to be obeyed. I choose to be a priest and put up with the celibacy rule. We received no real formation on celibacy: no explanations of the way it was linked to the priesthood; no history on how it developed within the Church. It just appeared like a rule added on. If you wanted to be a priest, then you had to put up with it.

At that time I thought that celibacy wasn't God's will. I have always believed that we should be continuously striving to get as close as possible to the early Church understanding, to living the Gospel message as the early Christians lived it. I knew that there were married priests in the early Church. But I was a full 20 years ordained, before I discovered that these married priests were expected to renounce the use of their marriage, and that this rule almost certainly went right back to the Apostles It now saddens me that the important and very conclusive evidence concerning this, was not given to me while I was studying for the priesthood.

I was deeply influenced by the fact that Jesus choose Peter, a married man. Since Jesus was happy to choose a married man, I felt that the Church should do the same. Indeed I felt that to oppose the practice of Jesus was to oppose the very will of God. The possibility that Peter had renounced the use of his marriage never entered my head, nor was it ever drawn to my attention.

I was ordained in 1974 when the real exodus from the priesthood was taking place. In 1974 alone, 3,464 priests left the priesthood.

It was an unsettling time.

There are those who complain about the way Pope John Paul 11 clamped down both on the debate about whether celibacy should be removed and on the procedures for priests being laicised. The statistics, however, indicate that Pope John Paul made a wise move.

In 1964, 640 priests left the ministry. Just five years later, 1969, the number leaving had jumped to 3,205. Three years later, 1972, the figure had risen to 3,729. So in eight years, it had gone from 640 to 3,729. It was almost a stampede! The majority didn't even seek to go through the procedures for laicisation. They just left.

After 1972, there was a slight decline in the numbers leaving. Pope Paul V1 was nearing the end. Many were waiting to see if a new Pope would make a change. There was a great expectation that he would.   All it required was a new Pope, they thought. Then, after the very brief reign of Pope John Paul 1, we got Pope John Paul 11. He did make a change, but not in the way expected. He declared that celibacy would stay. He declared that what appeared an endless debate about celibacy should be indeed ended.

He also ordered that the procedures for receiving laicisation should be greatly tightened. Many said that this would cause an increase in the numbers who left without asking for laicisation. The opposite proved the case. There was a steady drop in the numbers leaving, both of those who left seeking laicisation and of those who left without seeking laicisation. By 1984, the number leaving had dropped back to around 1,000 per year.

I was then a young priest who believed that celibacy was contrary to God's will, and Pope John Paul's approach did have a steadying impact. I could see that the rule wasn't about to be changed. I had enough spiritual formation to know that, even if celibacy wasn't God's most perfect will, that it was His will to work within the system.

I had been ordained in 1974. That was when the stampede was at its height.   A prominent priest, one that I looked up to and whose views I trusted, had then assured me that within ten years priests would be free to marry.

28/6/06.

A Protestant visionary was also 'receiving' messages that God wished for His sons (priests) be free to marry. I was given a copy of these messages. On the surface they appeared impressive.

So I know exactly what it is like to live as a young priest with,
A) The conviction that celibacy isn't God's will and,
B) The belief that it will soon go.

I must humbly admit that this had a detrimental effect on the earlier years of my priesthood, on the way in which I lived out the celibacy rule, on my emotional and spiritual development.

During this time I was also struggling sexually. My teenage experiences had left me a hurt person and this impacted on my entire person including my sexuality, but instead of being challenged to come to Jesus for healing and transformation, I was left with the frustrating belief that I was being asked to live a rule that was contrary to God's will. Later, by God's grace, I was to discover that one could experience immense sexual healing and deliverance, and that one could grow and grow in this healing until one truly becomes a free person sexually.

Sexual Healing

Jesus is as interested in our sexual healing as any other area of our being. He invites all people to entrust and consecrate their sexuality to Him in accordance with their vocation in life. He challenges all to flee from sexual immorality.

We priests and those who live the consecrated life are challenged to a life of total freedom, total sexual abstinence. Some seem to have a natural disposition for this. But for someone like myself, someone who has gone through a time of great personal brokenness, someone who has turned in upon himself, it doesn't come naturally and it isn't possible by will power. It is possible only by the grace of God, but by God's grace it is possible.

Jesus died on the cross to win for us the right to be free of our old selves, and part of our old self is sexual compulsion.
"Our old self was crucified with Him so that the sinful body might be destroyed, and we might no longer be enslaved to sin" Romans 6:6.
This is a most important element of the Good News:- that Jesus

has won for us the right to be free of our compulsions, that through Him we can be transformed. Indeed the very heart of the Good News is personal transformation through Jesus. Not merely is total sexual abstinence possible by God's grace but so too is total freedom; that is the state in which we have experienced such a degree of personal deliverance and healing, that it is no longer a struggle.

Firstly, with God's help, it is possible to live a life of sexual abstinence, difficult but possible. Then, through the prayer of desire, through being prayed with and through learning how to claim the healing which Jesus has won for us, it is possible to experience great sexual healing and deliverance, to be set free from compulsions.

I say to you, regardless of whether you are married or single, entrust your sexuality to God each day. Meditate on Scripture verses like,

"Shun sexual immorality. .... Do you not know that your body is a
temple of the Holy Spirit within you? ... You are not your own; you
were bought with a price. So glorify God in your body."
I Corinthians 6:18-20

Desire sexual healing, sexual deliverance. It is God's will for you. What He has done for me, He wishes to do for you too. If you have sexual compulsions, Jesus desires to heal you, to deliver you, to set you free. Mentally picture yourself being embraced by the love of God and being set free. Make this a top priority daily prayer. Go on asking and you will receive, go on seeking real freedom and you will find it, go on knocking on the door of sexual maturity and it will be granted on to you.

From burden to gift

Meanwhile so many of my brother priests live under the belief that celibacy isn't God's will. Many believe, as I once did, that the rule will go soon, that all it requires is a new Pope or a new Synod or a new Council. It is a terrible way to have to live.

Put simply, celibacy becomes a burden if one believes that it isn't God's will, and a double burden if one believes that not merely is it not God's will but that the rule will soon go.

Having been through it myself, I feel a deep sense of compassion for those priests who believe that celibacy isn't God's will and who expect that the rule will eventually go.

For them celibacy is liable to be a crippling and embittering experience. It will cast its shadow over fundamental areas of their life and priesthood. It has the potential to lead to grave sexual problems, to a spirit of rebellion against Church authority, to the impoverishment of their spiritual life, to perhaps their exit from the priesthood, and even to ongoing inner festering after they leave.

May I make it clear that, most often, it isn't celibacy itself that leads to these problems. It's the belief that celibacy isn't God's will, together with the expectation that it will go, that normally causes the deprivation, the impoverishment, the embitterment.

This is a most important distinction. I firmly believe that some have left the priesthood, who could have found great fulfilment in their priesthood, had they known the truth about how the priesthood was lived in the early Church. Instead they were given a falsified history by those agitating against celibacy and had the misfortune to believe that it was true.

I came through the tough way, but for me, today, celibacy is a most enriching experience. Not merely is that the way it is today, but it is the way it has been for many years. My celibacy not merely is not a burden but it brings a tremendous freedom. It allows me to open my whole life to God, to be filled with his love.

I can honestly say that I am so deeply in love with God, experience such a filling with His love, that it wouldn't be possible for me to fall in love or to become deeply emotionally involved with another person. Even before my experience of sexual healing, this was already so. I was still a divided person. In key areas I had still to experience the transforming power of the Gospel, but, while I was subject to sexual temptation, Jesus was already so deeply in the centre of my life that I was in no danger of 'falling in love'.

I still had a deep need for close friendship, and there was the danger that such friendships could become too intimate, but Jesus alone I loved. My emotions were already so centred on Him that I was incapable of falling in love with another person. Then, when I had my initial experience of sexual deliverance, it cleared the way for my relationship with Jesus to grow much deeper still, which in turn has given me a greater degree of inner personal strength.

I have gained a new capacity to love, a new capacity to be there for all people equally, a new capacity for non-possessive friendship, but my entire emotional being is centred on God. It would even be cruel for me to marry. If the lady had any form of possessive streak whatsoever, there would be a real conflict. She would come to see God as her rival, because He possesses my heart.

I accept that there are those who, either because of a deep seated tendency to loneliness or a deep rooted sexual problem, find celibacy a very difficult challenge. But remember I suffered both. I certainly suffered loneliness and inner emptiness to a most intense degree. This loneliness and inner emptiness came very close to destroying me. I hate to think of what might have been had I not been in the right place at the right time. Then, instead of destroying me, this emptiness left me open to a most powerful in-filling of God's love. Jesus truly became the Bread of Life for me.

I can only say:- be willing to seek Him where He can be found, and go on seeking Him until you do find. What He did for me, He desires to do for you also.

Paedophilia

Thankfully I never suffered tendencies towards paedophilia. I have never walked in the paedophile's shoes. I cannot speak for the person with this terrible affliction. But I know that Jesus loves the paedophile also.   What state of openness to God's love any particular paedophile is at, I cannot say. Is he like the prodigal son while the prodigal son still had his back turned on the father? The father still loved him, but this love was of no value to the son, until the son came to his senses and decided to go back to the father.

Some get so high on God's love and on God loving everyone that they forget this most important point. Of course God loves everyone!! Of course, His love continues while one sins. But, if through one's sin or one's disinterest, one has closed one's heart to God's love, then, unless one comes to one's senses and turns back to God, one has cut oneself off from His love.

But perhaps some paedophiles genuinely desire to serve God. Some may well be victims of their own compulsions. In his spirit, he may love Jesus. Jesus, however, is not Lord of a most important area of his life. Loving God, and desiring to serve Him, isn't enough for ministry. To be fit for ministry one needs to be able to incarnate His love; to be able to be the hands of Jesus, the voice of Jesus; to be able to bring something of the love of Jesus wherever one goes. This the paedophile cannot do while he remains in the control of his compulsions.

They say that paedophiles cannot change. I cannot accept that as the final word on the matter. The Bible says,

"Our old self was crucified with Him so that the sinful body might be destroyed" Romans 6:6.

This is a key element of the Gospel message, that Jesus has won for us the right to be free, that personal transformation is possible. This applies to the paedophile also. There must be a way, even if it hasn't yet been found. Jesus came to set prisoners free including those who are prisoners of their own compulsions.

So far, the process for coming into this deliverance has not been found. Perhaps it is because we have not been preaching the Good News. We have replaced the Gospel of Jesus Christ and the Good News of its transforming power by a religion centred on rituals from which we expect very little.

Jesus Himself outlined the implications of the Gospel.

"The Spirit of the Lord is upon me,
because he has anointed me to preach good news to the poor.
He has sent me to proclaim release to the captives
and recovering of sight to the blind,
to set at liberty those who are oppressed,
to proclaim the acceptable year of the Lord." Luke 4:18 -19

Today the poorest of the poor include paedophiles whose activities have been exposed. They are the real outcasts in our society, the real lepers, the untouchables. If we desire to walk in the shoes of Jesus, we must bring them good news, the hope of release from their captivity, the capacity to see the truth both about themselves and the love of Jesus for them.

Jesus desires His good news to be brought to all who suffer sexual difficulties. I suffered very deep sexual compulsions and I have been set free. God is fair. What He did for me, He desires to do for all. It is as easy for Jesus to deliver one from pneumonia as to deliver one from the flu. Since I experienced a miracle of sexual cleansing, it must also be possible for a paedophile.

But personal transformation does not happen by chance. It is most unlikely to happen unless one is willing to truly seek Jesus as the Bread of Life; unless one is prepared to seek to become open to Jesus and to have one's life transformed by Him with as much enthusiasm as an athlete will train for the Olympic Games.

Celibacy

Meanwhile it is not possible to truly live celibacy with resentment. It is not possible to truly live celibacy while working against it. This is a basic principle that applies not just to celibacy, but to any rule. If we are bound by a rule which we resent, it will impoverish us, possibly even destroy us. The secret in the case of celibacy, however, is not to get rid of the rule, but to discover the meaning of it, to discover the value behind the rule.

What a difference it has made for me to discover that while in the early Church they did have married priests, that these were expected to live a brother-sister relationship with their wives.

I used to believe that celibacy wasn't God's will based on what I knew of the early Church. Now, however, having been shown the evidence, I am deeply convinced that God's will and the teaching of Jesus demand a real separation from family.

In the Church founded by Jesus, there have, apart from a few special exceptions, been only two traditions for the living out of this separation:- in the first period married men were ordained on condition that they entered on a brother-sister relationship with their wives. In the second period, celibacy became the rule.

6

God's Radical Call

I have always experienced my call to the priesthood in a fairly radical way. At different times I investigated whether I should opt for a more radical form of religious life. At one stage I considered becoming a hermit. At another stage I considered trying to set up a house of prayer. Both are powerful callings. However, on each occasion, as soon as I started to take steps to bring about the plan, it became a mental pressure.

Each time, when I abandoned the plan, there was a sense of relief, nor was there any further sense of calling to either of the projects. With other projects, those to which God was calling me, the sense of call continued even at times when I put aside the plans.

When I went to Murrintown first, I felt that the house was too big, and that it conflicted with Jesus' call to leave all to follow him. One evening I looked up at it, and declared, "Lord, how can this be right?" An inner voice replied, "It is not that the house is too big. It is that you are too small!"

Later I came to need every bit of that house. For starters, when two separate people live in the one house, space is important. Then, when I started doing the Curate's Diary, extra space became very valuable. Indeed I ended up not merely having to convert the garage into a printing shed, but, when in Murrintown, to even replace the dining room sideboard with the collating-stapling machine.

God has called me to a more radical life within the framework that I have been given, rather than through leaving it. My calling is as a priest within the parish, but using that as a springboard for my ministry through the written word.

One thing I have found is that there is continuously a choice before me:- a choice between being willing to go the extra mile or staying where I am at. I have learned that whichever choice I make, the love of Jesus is there. But I have also learned that if I am to come under anointing, that if I am to see real blessings through my ministry, I need to go the extra mile.

Going the extra mile involved facing everything that needed to be faced in my own life. It involved seeking to grow and grow in my relationship with Jesus. It involved making quality time available for prayer each day. It involved being single-minded about doing the things that I felt Jesus was asking me to do.

When writing this book, the extra mile involved getting up regularly at 5.00am and working every hour that God gave me. I love going for walks, I love the beach, there are a host of other things that I could be doing. But right now I am sitting in front of my computer because I believe that that is where God is calling me to be.

Looking back I can see several different stages to my priesthood. Each time I managed to take a significant step in spiritual and moral growth, God's anointing upon my ministry became greater. When I grew in my relationship with Jesus, and He truly became Lord of key areas of my life, I experienced a deeper sense of joy and I also saw my ministry being blessed in greater ways. Jesus demanded a very radical lifestyle of his immediate disciples.

"If anyone comes to me and does not hate his own father and mother and wife and children and brothers and sisters, yes, and even his own life, he cannot be my disciple" Luke 14:26.

"Truly I say to you, there is no man who has left house or wife or brothers or parents or children, for the sake of the kingdom of God, who will not receive manifold more in this time, and in the age to come eternal life" Luke 18:29-30.

The call to full-time discipleship is truly radical. Jesus was totally uncompromising, used very blunt language. He left no room for half measures. Full-time ministry is no place for those who want the cosy life. Before experiencing the great joy, one must respond to the challenge.

The Wedding Feast

"A man once gave a great banquet, and invited many; and at the time for banquet he sent his servant to say to those who had been invited, 'Come; for all is now ready.' But they all alike began to make excuses. The first said to him, 'I have bought a field, and I must go out and see it; I pray you, have me excused.' And another said, 'I have bought five yoke of oxen, and I must go to examine them; I pray you, have me excused.' And another said, 'I have married a wife, and therefore I cannot come.' Luke 14:16-20

Here ordinary everyday activities, things which are normally important and valuable, are presented as a block to responding to God's call. Looking after one's animals, tending to one's land, spending time with one's spouse are important activities, part indeed of normal living. How then can they be obstacles to God's call for the ordinary Christian? Did Jesus not raise marriage to the dignity of a sacrament? Yet, here it is presented as an obstacle.

The parable of the Wedding Feast tells us that, for the Christian, nothing is more important than responding to the Gospel message, nothing must come before God in one's life; not one's property, not even one's family or one's spouse.

A healthy marriage has three partners, and God isn't the third partner - He is the first! This isn't because God punishes those who leave Him out of their lives. It is because we need God, and when we open our hearts to Him and to His way, we learn what it is to truly love. As one grows in one's relationship with Jesus, one receives an inner strength and also a greater capacity to love, to understand, to tolerate and to forgive.

But if the ordinary person is challenged to put God before property and even before marriage, how much more is the person who answers the call to full-time ministry so challenged? If one is to stand in the shoes of Jesus, there has to be a real renunciation of other options, a real willingness to leave property and family. The call to full time discipleship is so important that it not merely calls people to leave their businesses, it even calls them to leave family and marriage. Today there is great emphasis on the vocation of marriage being equal to the priestly vocation. I don't believe that it is right or even possible to compare vocations. It is for each person to answer God's call as it comes to them.

However, if one does insist on comparisons, the Biblical evidence is that Jesus spoke of a call that was so radical that it involved being willing to leave wife and family. Nobody was called to leave their ministry in order to marry. But the opposite was true. Jesus called his immediate disciples to leave everything, including home and family, to follow Him.

"The Husband of One wife"

Three times St. Paul uses the phrase "husband of one wife" in relation to ministry. On the surface this seems to give the green light to married priests and bishops. However when one begins to analyse the text more closely, a different picture begins to emerge.

"Now a bishop must be above reproach, the husband of one wife" 1 Timothy 3:2-3.

"Let deacons be the husband of one wife, and let them manage their children and their households well" 1 Timothy 3:12.

"Appoint elders in every town as I directed you, if any man is blameless, the husband of one wife, and his children are believers and not open to the charge of being profligate or insubordinate. For a bishop, as God's steward, must be blameless." Titus 1:5-7.

The phrase "the husband of one wife" is used in each of the three passages. The fact that St. Paul uses the precise same words on each occasion indicates that this was an accepted condition for becoming a priest, bishop or even deacon in the early Church. One had to be either the "husband of one wife" or else unmarried.

That, however, still doesn't tell us whether those who were married were free to live as husband and wife. Let us look deeper.

Scripture scholars accept that St. Paul wasn't just ruling out having two wives at the one time (polygamy). The early Church was very clear in its interpretation of this passage; that St. Paul was declaring that any man who remarried after the death of his first spouse wasn't eligible to become a priest, bishop or even a deacon, and that if a priest's wife died, he wasn't free to remarry.

Now why should this be? What was the thinking behind it? Is

there something here that isn't in writing? The Bible itself tells us that not everything was written down and that the people were to observe the teaching given by word of mouth as well as what was written.

So, if a priest was free to live a full conjugal relationship, why should he not be free to remarry if his wife died the day after his ordination? If he wasn't free to remarry if his wife died the day after his ordination, then is it not reasonable to raise the possibility that he wasn't free to have sexual relations either; the possibility that while he was married, he was expected to live as though he wasn't.

It may help us to understand the phrase "husband of one wife" if we look at what St. Paul says about widows. He recommends that younger widows should remarry (1 Timothy 5:14).

Older widows however could be enlisted in a special Church ministry known as "the Order of Widows" so long as they had been "the wife of one husband". Just as a man to be appointed priest, bishop or deacon had to be "the husband of one wife", so a widow in order to be appointed to the order of widows had to be "the wife of one husband".

Incidentally the order of widows exercised a ministry of intercessory prayer. See 1 Timothy 5:5. It is an order that could and should be revived but should be open to both men and women - people of mature age who are prepared to dedicate the rest of their lives to a ministry of intercessory prayer.

St. Paul says, "But refuse to enrol younger widows; for when they grow wanton against Christ they desire to marry, and so they incur condemnation for having violated their first pledge" 1 Tim. 5:11-12.

So once one was enrolled into the order of intercessory widows, one was not free to remarry. One was committed to a celibate life. Once again we have the connection between ministry, in this case a prayer ministry, and abstaining from marriage; indeed here between ministry and celibacy. Note the phrase "They grow wanton against Christ". In some way, their desire to remarry is a betrayal of their relationship with Christ. Their remaining celibate is an essential element of their calling. It would be better that they not join the intercessory order of widows than that they join and then desire to remarry.

Note also the word "pledge". In joining they made a "pledge". A key element of this pledge is to remain celibate. It introduces them to a new depth of relationship with Christ. He is now their real spouse. Thus, to break the pledge is to "grow wanton against Christ". To do so is a very serious matter. For this reason, St. Paul recommends that younger widows should seek to remarry rather than be enrolled, for, he says, "some have already strayed after satan" (1 Timothy 5:15). If this is what was asked of those joining the order of intercessory widows, what was asked of those who aspired to be priests and bishops?

The passage in Corinthians where Jesus speaks of the Church as "bride (of) one husband" is the only other place where he uses language similar to the phrase "husband of one wife" or "wife of one husband." It is not unreasonable to assume that the enrolled widow having to be the "wife of one husband" and the priest, bishop and deacon having to be the "husband of one wife" (or else unmarried) arises from the fact that the Church is the "bride (of) one husband". In other words it is because Jesus takes the Church as his bride.

In the case of the Order of Widows, the reason for their pledge was that they were taking Jesus as their spouse. The gap created by their widowhood was creating the space to come into a deeper relationship with Jesus, to focus on Him while interceding for the community, and, by their own lives, to witness to the great power of Jesus to enter lives, to fill the emptiness, and to bring strength.

Bishops, priests and deacons were also called to experience Jesus in a most special way as the Bread of Life, and to witness both in word and by their living, to the power of Jesus to enter one's life and transform it. But they were also called to go one step further. They were called to share in the ministry of Jesus who had taken the Church as His bride. There is but one Bridegroom, Jesus, but the priest is called to a special share in His ministry, called to serve as best man.

7

Living in Jesus

"He who eats my flesh my flesh and drinks my blood abides in me and I in him" John 6:56.

For 27 years I have known what it is to have Jesus live in me. This has been part of my lived experience. Even if I wake up in the middle of the night, I find myself in communion with Him. It is one of the wonderful blessings that come when the Holy Spirit dwells within us, a real ongoing relationship with Jesus, a tremendous sense of intimacy with Him, a wonderful experience of love for Him filling one's inner being. This has grown as I have grown in my openness to Him.

During the same 27 years, I have also been gradually learning what Jesus meant by eating His flesh and drinking His blood. These words mean far more than just receiving Him in Holy Communion. They mean opening ourselves to be transformed by Him. They mean having Jesus as Lord of every area of one's life. They mean living by His teaching, being moulded by His teaching. As we grow in this, our Baptism becomes a lived reality. We are truly flooded with the love of Jesus, penetrated by His light, dyed through and through by His love.

"All baptised in Christ, you have all clothed yourselves in Christ" Gal 3:27, (Jerusalem Bible).

Learning to truly eat His flesh and drink His blood is learning to live in Jesus. In a sense, to say that one is living in Jesus is such a total, all absorbing claim that one rightly shies away from making it. But one should not shy away from trying to live it; from the decision to seek to live totally and completely in Jesus. It is our very calling. It is part of Father's wonderful plan for us. It leads to a life that is filled with joy, ongoing breathtaking joy.

Opting for this is not a once-off decision, but rather one that needs to be made again and again. It is one that has to be lived each day, one day at a time. First one must seek a personal relationship with Jesus, must seek to have Jesus as one's best Friend. Then one entrusts one's life to Him, what has traditionally been called consecrating oneself to the Sacred Heart - or should I say, one invites Jesus to consecrate us to His Sacred Heart, as this is something that He alone can do; only God can consecrate.

Again being consecrated to His Sacred Heart involves far more than a mere prayer formula. True consecration demands that we face up to what needs to be faced within us. That which is contrary to God's will cannot be consecrated to Him. Bitterness, hateful feelings, judgmentalism, lust, covetousness:- none of these things can be consecrated to God, nor does one truly live in Jesus until one has begun to renounce all these things.

Ongoing Inner Healing

True consecration, to truly live in Jesus demands a major inner transformation, a real rebirth. It demands that one opens every area of one's mind and heart to the cleansing power of Jesus. It demands that one opens up all one's memories to Him, renounces wrong choices and wrong responses, and seeks ongoing inner healing and, where necessary, deliverance.

When we look at the stars, we see them not as they are today, but as they were millions of years ago. It takes their light millions of years to reach the earth. So, when we look into the night sky, we are looking at what existed millions of years ago. Jesus is eternal. If we can look at what existed millions of years ago, how easy it is for Him to go back with us to what happened 10, 20, 30, 40, 50, 60 or even 70 years ago. Indeed because He is eternal, He is outside time and can reach into what, to us, is in the past.

Jesus desires to walk back in time with us, to go back with us to times when we were deeply hurt and to bring healing into those hurts. He was already there when we were suffering, but, perhaps, we hadn't a deep relationship with Him. He was there, but He couldn't help us in coping with the hurt as He hadn't yet become Lord of our spirits.

Now however, as we allow Him to truly live in us, we can invite Him to walk right back in time with us. We can become conscious of the situation in which we were hurt, and literally allow Jesus to hold our hand. One does so by calling to mind the incident, then mentally seeing Jesus step into the situation. In one's mind's eye one sees Jesus being there at the moment one was suffering, lifting one up, giving one strength, bringing healing, and enabling one to feel deeply loved and accepted.

If you feel deep shame, it is important to realise that Jesus really loves you, that He understands everything, that your hurt is also His hurt, that He desires to cleanse you and to take away the shame. No matter what was done to you or what you did to others, Jesus will NEVER turn His back on you, but if you suffer deep shame, your inner mind may try to tell you that He will. In your mind's eye, you may even see Jesus turning away. If that happens, do NOT believe it.

Indeed if that happens, it just shows how much you need inner cleansing and the healing of memories. It may also show that somehow, through the hurt, satan has gained a toehold in your mind. Do not be frightened even by that. Jesus is far stronger than satan and He desires to set you free. Keep inviting Jesus to be Lord over this area of your mind, and keep telling satan that he has no right to hurt you in this way.

We are fond of inviting Jesus to go back with us in time to heal the hurts. We must also invite Him to go back with us in time to where we made wrong choices and developed wrong attitudes, and wrong ways of responding and behaving. This is a truly necessary step for rebirth. Become conscious of when you started making a particular wrong response, call the situation to mind, including why you started responding in this way, then invite Jesus to deliver you from this way of responding. Mentally picture Him enabling you to respond appropriately.

Jesus desires to go back with us in time to the moment of our conception, and to redeem every moment, to transform every moment, to penetrate every moment with His light. Until this happens our Baptism isn't quite complete, for to be truly baptised is to be flooded with His presence, dyed through and through by His love, penetrated by His light.

Surrender of the will

Living in Jesus involves entering into an extraordinary relationship with Him, a relationship of continuous intimacy. For this to happen, one needs to make a real surrender of one's life and one's will to God and to his way of thinking.

Our will needs to be brought into tune with the divine will. This involves a major handing over, a major new attitude, a new way of thinking, a real surrender. Nor is this something that one can be successful in, on one's own. It is a case of us asking, seeking, knocking, and trusting in God to enable us to surrender our will to His. If, in reading this, you decide for the very first time to seek to surrender your will to God, pause and sit back. Then allow your mind to form a mental image of itself, that is of your mind and your will. Then picture yourself entrusting all this, entrusting your very mind to be penetrated and permeated by the mind of God.

Take your time, repeating the exercise, sitting back, allowing into your mind an image of itself, then picturing your mind being surrendered to God, and penetrated and permeated by His light.

Even if you are pleased with the exercise, don't expect it to take great effect at once. It needs to be repeated hundreds of times, and lived in the difficult moments as well as in the smooth ones.

Hold down the branch of a tree and it will remain in the down position just as long as you hold it down. When you let go, it will swing back up to its original position. But if it is kept tied down, it will eventually be trained to stay down. So too with the mind. At first, it will remain surrendered to the will of God just while you seek to surrender it - and maybe not even that long! But, as one perseveres, one trusts that the Holy Spirit will accept one's offering, will accept one's attempts to surrender one's will, one's attempts to live and breathe the will of God.

Then one must begin to live the surrender in everyday situations. It is one thing to entrust your will during prayer time, it is yet another to begin to live that out in the midst of the ups and downs of everyday life. How often have we prayed for the grace to do things God's way, then five minutes later completely forgotten our prayer when something intruded upon us!

From the time we first receive the grace to make the prayer of surrender, until that surrender is reflected in our ongoing reactions, a process of growth, healing and transformation is required.

Jesus needs to truly become Lord of every area of one's life. This requires ongoing inner conversion, a willingness to repent of every thought and attitude that is self orientated. How can the arrogant surrender their will to God before healing and repentance has taken place? How can the stubborn, the self-willed, the rebellious? How can those with a compulsive need to prove themselves? How can those who are bitter or fighting with their neighbours? How can the person with unresolved hurts? How can the person who has sexual compulsions or is in wrong relationships? How can anyone who is prey to any form of compulsion? Nor is it easy for those who desire to be dependent, who desire to cling. God is our only sure dependence and it is upon Him alone that one must depend. One's dependence on God needs to be greater and clearer than on any person.

Yet Jesus is forever willing to work with us where we are at. Even when what is required is harder than for a camel to pass through the eye of a needle, He will still work with us. Even if there is still inner turmoil in one's life, even if one is still a split person, even if one is still struggling, Jesus will work with us.

Don't miss out

Jesus has been very patient with me through many years of struggles and failures, though He has also been impatient with me when I needed a further push. I give thanks to Jesus both for His patience and His impatience. I also look back and think of how things could have been different had I responded more fully earlier:- how

I could have been a better priest, how I could have helped more people, how I could have avoided causing hurt, and how my own life could have been full of the joy and happiness earlier.

It's a sobering thought. When one is slow to respond to Jesus, one is missing out. One isn't the person that God desires one to be, nor does one experience what God desires one to experience. This impacts on one's family and on one's loved ones. Not merely will one not bring the level of blessing that God desires one to bring into their lives, but one may well bring hurt, even serious hurt.

If you really wish to experience the touch of the Holy Spirit, to see the fruit of the Holy Spirit being released in your life, to become a source of blessing to your family and your community, then take the steps necessary to be transformed by Jesus!

Each year I attend the Intercession for Priests. Normally I receive the opportunity to meet Sr. Briege McKenna there. She shares with me some mental images and then gives a passage or two of Scripture to meditate on. One year she gave me John 11:1-44, the account of the raising of Lazarus for the dead. I read it, but it meant nothing to me. Well, I reckoned, she can't always be inspired! The following year I went back again, and guess the passage she gave me! John 11:1-44!

However on this occasion, she shared images that came to her concerning how the passage applied to me; that just as Jesus came to the tomb of Lazarus and raised him from the dead, that so too He was standing before me desiring to touch the areas of deadness within me and to bring me into a further experience of the new life, resurrected life.

The truth is that Jesus was living in me for many years while I was still only partly living in Him. I was proclaiming Him Lord, but there were areas of my life of which He wasn't Lord. While this is so, not merely is there a limit to the extent to which His power and His love can flow within us, but there is also a great limit both on the extent to which we can be his hands and voice and on the extent to which our ministry will be under anointing. I can see now that, for many years, my own ministry was a bit like an apple tree that had been full of bloom, only to be hit by a late frost. The fruit was scarce.

Sometimes if things are not going well in a parish or a diocese, it is at least legitimate to ask if there is something amiss within the leadership, something that could be a block to God's blessings.

If we desire ministries that come under God's anointing, there is only one way - personal transformation, personal purification, personal holiness amongst those in leadership. We may fool people, but we won't fool God. Indeed very often, we don't fool people either. They can sense when something is wrong even when they don't quite know what it is.

The challenge to personal transformation is at the heart of the Good News. That personal transformation is possible, is indeed a key element of the Good News. Yet we need a patient firmness as we encourage and challenge people. Life is a journey, a pilgrimage, an opportunity for growth. All this takes time. Sometimes a person may need some time and some space. But the shorter the time it takes for one to respond, the better not just for oneself but also for one's family and the community, yet we must be patient even as Jesus is patient.

In reaching out to others, we need to take on the mind of Jesus:- to seek to love as He loves, to understand as He understands, to encourage as He encourages, to have His strength, His courage, His patience and indeed eventually His impatience! Our calling is not to condemn, but rather to affirm and recognise the steps that others have taken, just as over the years Jesus affirmed and recognised our steps.

Bringing blessing to others

Those who truly learn to live in Jesus will become a mighty source of blessing for both their family and the wider community. The Bible promises that not merely will one's own family be blessed, but even one's children's children.

"His righteousness (is) to children's children to those who keep his covenant and remember to do his commandments" Psalm 103:18.

One person, Jesus, redeemed the whole world by perfectly living God's will. He was able to do this because He was truly God as well as truly man. Yet, just think - because one person truly lived God's will, the entire world was redeemed. Infinite graces not merely flowed then, but continue to flow and will flow forever.

This should give us great hope. We are not Jesus, but Jesus desires to live in us and invites us to live in Him. When this truly happens, great blessings flow. When we in truth 'eat His flesh and drink His blood'; when we bring to our participation in the daily Eucharist, lives that are truly being lived in Jesus, wills that are constantly seeking surrender to God's will, blessings flow.

Jesus, one man, by living God's will totally, brought infinite blessings. We can be the conduit for a flow of these blessings to our vicinity. If we live in Jesus! If we in truth 'eat His flesh and drink His blood'.

When even a small group of transformed people join in daily Mass, great blessings are released. I believe, for example, that where such a group exists and where they offer a brief prayer for God's protection at daily Mass, that the number of tragedies in their area could be cut by at least 30% and possibly 75%. There is, of course, no guarantee. Nobody has that. I could be dead before you even read this!

The greatest blessing of all is coming to live in Jesus. That is the greatest blessing we can bring people. We must never give up on praying that others may experience Jesus as we have experienced Him, never give up on inviting others to join us. Even if 100 fail to respond, we must continue to invite.

Think of how my life was transformed because a young student, Joe Ralph, gave me a copy of the Cross and the Switchblade, and because Benny McHale invited me to a Prayer Meeting. Because two people reached out to me, I am now experiencing a truly fabulous joy-filled life, and can in turn reach out to others.

If even one in every thousand we invite respond, our time will have been very well spent and we will have been instrumental in something truly awesome.

8

Learning to "Do THIS"

Could you imagine being at a wedding where they just made the icing and didn't bother with the cake? Yet in a very real sense, that is what we have done with the Mass for most of the past 2,000 years. All because we have failed to understand the meaning and significance of two simple words, "Do this".

During World War Two in Trent in Italy, a group of young ladies started to bring a Bible with them to the air-raid shelters and to meditate on its meaning. It was a time of great danger and they were trying to live the Gospel message in that situation.

One day they were discussing John 15:13, "Greater love has no man than this, that a man lay down his life for his friends." They discussed whether they would be willing to lay down their lives for their friends. Then they made a very special pact, committing themselves to be willing to lay down their lives for one another. They did the round of the circle, looking into each other's eyes and declaring, "I am prepared to lay down my life for you."

The leader of that group of teenagers and young adults was Sylvia Lubich. She later took the name Chiara Lubich when consecrating her life to God. Chiara has remained single and celibate. Her leadership is a very real sharing in the priesthood of Jesus, a life of total self-giving, nothing held back or reserved. Today (1999) she continues to live the consecrated single life.

Chiara didn't set out to start a movement. The movement just started around her. In a very real sense, the defining moment was that occasion when they each looked into one another's eyes and declared, "I am prepared to die for you." That was the moment that changed their group, from being a nice cosy little group of young people who met to talk about the Bible, into the nucleus of a group that would have a major impact on the Church and the world. After that, people just started flocking to them and still continue to do so today, fifty years later. Eventually they took the name, "Focolare". Today the Focolare Movement has four million members - which is as many members as there are citizens in Switzerland. This all started when a group of young girls looked into each other's eyes and declared, "I am prepared to die for you." What they did was similar to what Jesus did at the Last Supper - except, of course, that He didn't just declare that He was willing to die for His friends:- He declared that He actually was going to die for them. He looked into the apostles' eyes and declared, "This is my body which will be given up for you" Luke 22:19.

That is what Jesus was speaking of when He asked the apostles to "Do THIS". He was asking for people who would be ready to lay down their lives and to live their lives for Him and for one another.

What Chiara and her young friends did was highly Eucharistic. They were responding in a special way to Jesus' instruction, "Do THIS". Every time we go to the altar to celebrate Mass, we are called to do the same.

At Mass, we priests are called to look into the eyes of our people and to declare, "I am prepared to die for you. I am going to give my life in your service." Living this himself in a very radical way through his celibate dedication, the priest can then invite his people to also share in it. The people are not called to the same level of total and exclusive self-giving to the entire community. But yet they too are called to be part of it; called to look into each other's eyes and declare, "I am prepared to die for you."

There is a twofold direction in the Mass. Firstly, Jesus is offering Himself to His Father, offering Himself completely and totally. It is the greatest love offering that there has ever been. Secondly, Jesus' offering of His life was in a special way for us.

In saying, "Do THIS", He invites us to unite ourselves with His offering of Himself to His Father, to become immersed in that offering, and secondly to look into each other's eyes and declare, "I am willing to die for you. I offer up my life for you."

When this begins to happen, then the Eucharist will truly begin to be celebrated, and when the Eucharist truly begins to be celebrated, then new life will begin to enter the Church.

A total offering of self

For the Last Supper, Jesus only had the twelve present. It was the one special occasion when he had the full twelve and nobody but the twelve. That too is significant. This occasion was reserved for those who were about to be asked to stand in His shoes. It was to them in the first place that the words, 'Do THIS' were addressed.

They were the ones who were to take His place after His death. They were to 'Do THIS', that is unite themselves to His total offering of Himself to His Father, commit their lives totally to it, be willing to lay down their lives for their people, and then, having entered into deep union with His self-giving, repeat His act of consecration of the bread and wine.

Just as Jesus was giving even His very life for us, so too they were being called to give themselves in a special way in life and in death for His people. They were called to a living and radical union with Jesus' total self-giving. Only then would they truly "do THIS"; only then could they truly stand in His place; only then would they be fit ministers of the consecration of the bread and wine.

The call of Jesus to those who would stand in His shoes is radical, brutally radical. He used language designed to leave nobody in doubt of how radical it was.

"If anyone comes to me and does not hate his own father and mother and wife and children and brothers and sisters, yes, and even his own life, he cannot be my disciple." Luke 14:26

While the word 'hate' in the original Aramaic had a different nuance to our word 'hate', it left no doubt about the response demanded of those being called to 'Do THIS'. One had to be prepared to give oneself, totally, completely, without any hold back. There had to even be a real break with family ties and commitments so as to be available for all.

We see this in Jesus' own life. Not merely was He celibate, but there also was a break with His own family as a human institution. His mother and His brethren were 'outside', Mark 3:31.

Every time I go to the altar, I am deeply conscious that I am called to do far more than just consecrate the bread and wine; that I am called to 'Do THIS' in a much fuller sense. There is no true "Do THIS" unless I as a priest am offering myself totally and completely in union with the sacrifice of Jesus to Father for all God's people, and in particular for those entrusted to my care.

Sometimes one may have negative feelings towards a person or persons. Sometimes one may feel annoyed or angry. But when one stands at the altar, when one is offering up the sacred species, they are the people one should be thinking of first and foremost. One is offering oneself, offering up one's life and energy for them too.

Unlike Jesus, few of us have to die for our people. Instead we are called to live for them. Our offering of ourselves should be seen in the way we live, a life of dedicated service. When one pronounces the words,

"Take this, all of you and eat it;
this is my body which will be given up for you,"

one is speaking in the first place of the action of Jesus. But one is only fulfilling the command of Jesus, 'Do THIS' if one is truly standing in the place of Jesus, offering up one's whole life in union with Him to Father.

There should be a very deep union between the words of consecration and the personal consecration by the priest of his own life. In saying, "Take this" he is speaking of what Jesus is doing, and also of his own self-giving in union with Jesus.

In saying, "This is my body which will be given up for you", he is again speaking in the person of Jesus, but it shouldn't be just the body of Jesus that is offered. The priest's own self-offering should be in total union. As he unites with the self-offering of Jesus, he offers his own life in conjunction. The same applies with the

chalice. When the priest pronounces the words of consecration,
"Take this, all of you, and drink from it:
this is the cup of my blood, the blood of the new and everlasting
covenant. It will be shed for you and for all so that sins may be
forgiven,"
there should again be a deep union between the priest's personal
self-offering and the offering of Jesus. In his heart the priest should
be saying to his people, "I am giving my life for you. I am giving
my life in union with the self-giving life and death of Jesus; all
that I am and all that I have I offer to the Father in union with
Jesus' self-offering."

Having then made this offering himself, the priest invites the people
to a similar offering according to their station in life.

A Great Privilege

When we celebrate Mass, the Last Supper is made present, Jesus'
complete offering of Himself to Father on Calvary is made present,
and the Risen Jesus comes to meet us. Mind they are not repeated,
they are made present. We have the opportunity to join the Apostles
in the Upper Room, to join Our Lady and St. John beneath the
cross, and to have the Risen Jesus make His home within us. What
a privilege!

We also have the opportunity to join with Jesus in His offering
of Himself to Father and the challenge to look into each other's
eyes and declare, 'I am willing to lay down my life for you.'

Celebrating the Mass or participating in it, is a tremendous
privilege. Even thinking about it fills my heart with joy. There is
so much happening in the Mass - one just can't take it all in at
once.

But it is also a tremendous challenge. We are not merely called
to allow Jesus to dwell in us, but also to literally stand in His
place at the key moment of His self-giving to Father made present
in the consecration of the Mass. We can only truly stand in His
place if we have first been transformed by Him.

For us priests in particular, our very vocation is to stand in the place of Jesus; to stand in the place of Him who had no other bride but the Church, to serve daily as His best man. But it isn't just the priest who is called to something truly special in the Mass. We are all called not just to be united with Jesus' offering, not just to stand in the place of Jesus, but to become the living presence of Jesus in today's world.

In Baptism we are called to be flooded with Jesus. In the Mass we are called to be His living presence. This, of course, requires ongoing transformation; that we do not stop until every area of our being has been penetrated by the light and love of Jesus so that the words of Jesus may truly be fulfilled,

"He who eats my flesh and drinks my blood has eternal life, and I will raise him up on the last day. For my flesh is food indeed and my blood is drink indeed. He who eats my flesh and drinks my blood abides in me, and I in him." John 6:54-55

When we enter the Mass in this spirit, great blessings are released.

Footnote 1 - Abusing the Mass

The Mass is about becoming united with Jesus' self-offering to Father, about being immersed into Jesus, about offering to lay down our lives for one another. It is a truly sacred occasion.

How often we belittle it with a profusion of collections, with long winded sermons, with both preaching and then reading a lengthy letter or turning the announcements into further sermons. We need to learn that nothing, nothing, nothing, should come before the celebration of the Mass or be allowed to distract from it.

It is the place for God's agenda, not ours; for enabling people to become united with the offering of Jesus to Father, enabling them to truly meet Jesus as the Bread of Life, enabling them to let go of selfishness and to enter into a love commitment. It is not the place for personal agendas. So too with the Church Calendar and its feastdays. Letters about unrelated matters and visiting preachers who ignore the meaning of the feastday should both be banned on feastdays, including such important feasts as the Baptism of Jesus, Mercy Sunday, the Ascension and Corpus Christi. These feastdays are given to us to enable us to become more open to the wonderful new life that Jesus offers and they should not be hijacked for other agendas, however noble.

Footnote 2 - The connection between celebrating the Eucharist and continence

The connection between the priest's sexual abstinence and celebrating the Eucharist goes back to the very early Church. But so often, even in relatively early years, it was wrongly perceived to derive from attitudes towards sex itself. It derives instead from the total self-giving given in the first place by the celibate, Jesus, and demanded by Him of His special disciples, the priests.

The priest is called to give of himself in a very radical way, totally, completely, with nothing held back. Because it is a total self-giving, it is also an exclusive self-giving. That is why it demands either celibacy or a form of renunciation of marriage.

There is an inherent clash between the totality with which the priest is invited to offer himself in the Mass and the totality with which one is supposed to give oneself in marital union. Giving oneself in sexual union is also designed to be a total self-giving. It is also designed to be an exclusive self-giving. It is an expression of one's commitment to put that person first and before all others. Hence there is an incompatibility between the two.

One cannot at the same time give oneself totally and completely to one person and to God's people. Both are meant to be total. Both are meant to be exclusive.

Footnote 3 - The relationship between the Last Supper and the Crucifixion

The Passover Meal which Jesus began with his disciples was not completed in the Upper Room. During the Passover Meal the cup should have been passed around 4 times, but Jesus and the apostles left after the third cup.

The third cup at the Passover Meal was known as the Cup of Blessing. This is the cup over which Jesus pronounced the words of institution,

"This is my blood of the covenant which is poured out for many".
"Truly, I say to you, I shall not drink again of the fruit of the vine until that day when I drink it new in the kingdom of God" Mark 14:24 -25.

Note that Jesus consistently used the phrase "kingdom of God" to refer to the emergence of God's kingdom on earth, so "when I drink it new in the kingdom of God" could well involve drinking it here on earth. But if Jesus and His disciples left after the third cup, the Cup of Blessing, they didn't drink the fourth cup, the Cup of Completion. Why?

Jesus went to the Garden of Gethsemane. There He prayed,

"Remove this cup from me" Mk. 14:36.

What cup was he referring to? Was it the Cup of Completion? Had it become identified with the Cross? Was the Cross the Cup of Completion"

Before nailing Him to the Cross, they tried to give Jesus "wine mixed with a drug called myrrh but Jesus would not drink it" (Mk. 15:23). Then, just as he was about to die,

Jesus cried out "I thirst". Someone soaked a sponge in the wine, put it on a branch of hyssop, and lifted it to his lips. Jesus took the wine and said, 'It is finished!' Then He bowed His head and died.
John 19:29-30 (Paraphrased).

The word 'finished' could also be translated as 'completed' or 'consummated'. The 'Cup of Completion' had now been drunk. It was only with His death on the cross that the Last Supper was truly completed.

There are also several other links between Jesus' death and the Passover Meal. St. John tells us that it was the sixth hour when Jesus died. This was the hour at which the High Priest sacrificed the Passover Lamb.

Not one of his bones were broken - only a lamb that never had a broken bone could be sacrificed for the Passover Meal.

The High Priest wore a seamless garment when celebrating the Passover. Jesus wore a seamless garment on his way to crucifixion showing that He was at once high priest as well as the sacrificial lamb.

The high Priest used a hyssop stick to sprinkle the blood. A hyssop stick was used to give Jesus the 'fourth cup'.

All this has importance for the celebration of the Mass. The Last Supper started in the Upper Room. It ended on the cross. In it we have the total self-giving of Jesus. In the Mass, the Last Supper is made present, Jesus' offering of Himself on Calvary is made present and the Risen Jesus comes to us in Holy Communion.

For an in-depth study of the question of the Fourth Cup, see Scott Hahn's new book, "A Father who keeps His promises", published by Servant Publications.

9

Being the hands of Jesus

Jesus works through incarnation, that is through people who are willing to be His living presence in the world. We are all called to be the hands of Jesus, the feet of Jesus, the voice of Jesus; to bring something of the love of Jesus and the joy of the Holy Spirit wherever we go. He has no other hands but ours. In a most literal sense He has placed His mission in our hands. This is at once an awesome realisation and a wonderful calling. And it is for everybody! Every person is called to be the living presence of Jesus in the world.

We priests and all in Christian leadership, including parents, are, in a special way, called to be the living presence of Jesus in the way we relate to our people. Offering to give our lives for them in the Mass, we have to learn to live our lives for them each day in a spirit of caring love.

If the ordinary person falls down on living out their calling, it may not be that noticeable and the damage may be limited, but when we priests fail to be the voice of Jesus, the hands of Jesus, we are a real contradiction. Our ministry is dysfunctional.

Yet not one of us is perfect when ordained. We are ordinary human beings. We too suffered hurts in our early life. We too have to learn how to come into the healing that Jesus offers. We too have to learn the true meaning of Christian love, agape self-giving love. We too have to grow and to continue to grow both in our personal relationship with Jesus and in our capacity to minister His love.

I must humbly admit that when I was ordained there was a lot of hurt and anger still within me. When there is hurt and anger within, it affects the way in which one sees reality, the way in which one responds to people. One is judgemental, tending to see things in terms of black and white, going over the top when faced with opposition, taking things very personally, worrying and losing sleep over things, running around in circles.

One may also have a compulsion to prove oneself, a compulsion to have one's work recognised, perhaps even to be seen to be better than others. This can lead to an enormous amount of energy being used up in promoting oneself rather than promoting Jesus Christ and His kingdom.

Yet it is good that we priests have to face these things. If we didn't have to learn ourselves, we wouldn't be able to teach others. Every insight in this book has been learned in the school of personal experience. Our problems are turned into blessings when, through Jesus, we gain victory over them.

To Love As God Loves

"Love is of God, and he who loves is born of God and knows God. He who does not love does not know God; for God is love" 1 John 4:7-8.

"God is love and he who abides in love, abides in God, and God abides in him" 1 John 4:16.

These lines have a magical ring about them. Everybody loves them yet few understand their full meaning, much less live them. St. John wasn't speaking of romantic love or even platonic love, but of agape love, the self-giving love that keeps on loving regardless of the response and regardless of the cost. He was speaking of the type of love that enables one to love as God loves. This type of love is most challenging. For its fulfilment, there can no longer be a bitter, compulsive or selfish bone left in our bodies.

St. Paul spells it out in 1 Corinthians 13:1-13. It doesn't matter what other spiritual gifts one has, if one hasn't this type of love they have no value, he says. One can be a real miracle worker, but without a capacity for selfless love, one is nothing. One can even give away everything one has but if one isn't loving in one's relationships, it is useless.

St. Paul possibly learned this the hard way. On his first visit to

Jerusalem after his conversion, he spoke "boldly", so boldly in fact that the Greek speaking Jews wanted to kill him. Paul had never been one to do things by half. Previously he had sought to have all Christians thrown in prison. Then he had his conversion experience, but he was in many ways still the same person.

Soon his method of preaching had stirred up serious trouble, unnecessary trouble. As a result he had to be rescued and sent to Tarsus. The next verse after the account of Paul being sent to Tarsus, reads, "So it was that the Church throughout Judaea, Galilee and Samaria had a time of peace" Acts 9:31, (GN). The Church had a time of peace, that is, after Paul was given a holiday. He has the distinction of being the first Christian minister to be sent on administrative leave!

It appears that the administrative leave may have been quite prolonged, possibly 14 years. During this time, Paul was living quietly in Tarsus and presumably maturing, growing in his capacity to love, facing his own compulsions. There isn't even a mention of him being involved in public ministry there. Eventually, when the timing was right, that is when God knew he was ready, he was sent for again. "Barnabas went to Tarsus to look for Paul" Acts 11:25. Note how it says "to look for Paul". This suggests that Paul was living in obscurity; Barnabas had to look for him.

Paul, the most famous Christian missionary of all time, had to wait patiently for the call to come. He had to await the Lord's timing. Meanwhile he had to face the demons within himself, had to learn how to become open to the Lord's transforming power, had to learn the meaning of love. It is because he learned for himself that he is such a good teacher. He says,

"Love is patient and kind; love is not jealous or boastful; it is not
arrogant or rude. Love does not insist on its own way; it is not
irritable or resentful; it does not rejoice at wrong, but rejoices in the
right. Love bears all things, believes all things, hopes all things,
endures all things." 1 Corinthians 13:4-7

If you are truly incarnating love, it will be possible to replace the word love in this passage with your own Christian name, "X is patient and kind; X is not jealous or boastful; X is not arrogant or rude. X does not insist on his own way; X is not irritable or resentful; X does not rejoice at wrong, but rejoices in the right. X bears all things, believes all things, hopes all things, endures all things."

Very few enter adulthood with much capacity for this type of love. The first big step is when one makes a commitment to love and to building up God's kingdom. This is a most important step, an absolutely necessary one without which no real progress may be made. But even where a person has made this commitment, a great transition has still to take place before one is capable of agape love. In my early ministry I had reached the stage where I really sought to love, to reach out the helping hand, to be there for people. I was very committed to this. However if I felt that people weren't nice in return or if they criticised me, I responded negatively. If their reaction was hostile or aggressive, so too was my response. It never even struck me that what I was doing was wrong!

Jesus calls us to a deeper type of love, to go the extra mile.
"If you love those who love you, what credit is that to you? For even sinners love those who love them" Luke 6:32.

"But I say to you that hear, Love your enemies, do good to those who hate you, bless those who curse you, pray for those who abuse you. To him who strikes you on the cheek, offer the other also; and from him who takes away your cloak do not withhold your coat as well" Luke 6:27-29.

When someone wrongs us and we find that a prayer asking God to bless them is rising automatically in our hearts, then we know that our spirit is under the prompting of the Holy Spirit and that we are beginning to live the type of love to which Jesus calls us.

But that is not something that happens easily or that one can come into overnight. The human instinct is to fight back, to curse those who stand in one's way, to answer insult with insult. Jesus challenges us to move from that primitive form of responding to a life of love that is based on Father's love.

Along the way, not merely will any inner anger have to be dealt with, but also a lot of dying to self has to take place. As long as self is instinctively more important to one than living God's love, one will lash back. In one's earlier years, while one may be very committed to Jesus and to His teaching, self is also very important. One will have a real need to know that one is doing okay, a real need to achieve and to be appreciated. In its extreme forms, this can lead to a need to win or to be seen to be better than others, or a need to be in control.

Criticism, opposition and anything that appears an insult is a real challenge to that inner need. It hits one where it hurts. One feels a need to fight back, to overcome, even to destroy the opposition. But one cannot truly be open to the Holy Spirit while this continues.

Much mellowing has to take place. This involves looking at whatever anger and negative emotions that one may have, including anger towards oneself, exploring its roots, and then taking the steps necessary to reach the stage where one can forgive and let go. The person who hasn't learned to forgive will not be capable of Christ-like love. As long as there is unresolved anger within a person, it will find an object:- there will always be someone to hate or to dislike.

By unresolved anger, I mean in the first place, anger that hasn't even been faced; that hasn't been acknowledged as needing to be challenged and dealt with. The person with this type of anger is locked into their anger, failing to see how destructive and self-limiting it is; perhaps even failing to acknowledge that it even exists, certainly failing to face up to the hurt their anger is causing.

Sometimes the anger may go back to a repressed memory in early childhood or even to something that happened in infanthood that cannot now be recalled. Sometimes it may even be inherited or picked up from one's family. Sometimes a tendency for anger may be evident in several generations of the one family, and will likely continue until someone takes responsibility for breaking the cycle. Sometimes all that one knows is that there is unexplained anger or judgmentalism continuously erupting.

If one has inner anger that hasn't been even acknowledged much less faced one will NOT take Jesus' teaching on love seriously. One will see it as an impossible ideal that one can ignore. Or, at least, one feels it doesn't apply to one's own situation. One ends up seeing no inconsistency between being a Christian and holding even strong bitterness, dislikes and judgmentalism.

Jesus knew that not everybody was ready for agape love, the type of selfless loving to which He was calling them. He said, "I say to you that hear, Love your enemies" Luke 6:27. Jesus knew that not everyone would have ears to hear. Many would be deaf to his teaching. So it was and so it is.

But it isn't just anger toward others that needs to be faced if one is to become truly open to agape love. Part of the anger that requires facing is anger towards self; anger that manifests itself in feelings of inferiority and inadequacy. It isn't easy to truly love someone if one feels either inferior or superior to them.

An important step towards a capacity for selfless love is to recognise the equality of all before God. This includes every person, including the street children, the richest millionaires, our colleagues and our superiors. Each is of equal value in the eyes of Father. Each is a precious person for whom Jesus died.

So too, those responsible for bringing hurt or disappointment into our lives, and those who have traditionally been seen as the enemy of our country, club or family are equally loved by Father. Each is a precious person for whom Jesus died. Including also those of whom we most thoroughly disapprove, people who may have done the most reprehensible things!

Often, if a person has done something really bad, the first reaction is to see them as a monster, to seek to besmirch everything that they have ever done or stood for. Sometimes the demonisation is a phase that may need to be worked through, an understandable part of the anger. But, in the long run, not merely is it not the Christian approach, it slows healing and may even prevent it altogether.

Once one learns to see the culprit or abuser as a human being with a terrible sickness, one is on the road to healing; to see him or her as a precious person for whom Jesus died; a person who himself or herself needs to be rescued. When the Spirit of the Lord is truly upon us, we will desire to see them set free of their hatred and compulsions rather than seeing them punished, destroyed.

At the beginning of His public ministry, Jesus, reading from the Prophet Isaiah, declared,

> *"The Spirit of the Lord is upon me,*
> *because he has anointed me to preach good news to the poor.*
> *He has sent me to proclaim release to the captives,*
> *and recovery of sight to the blind,*
> *to set at liberty those who are oppressed,*
> *to proclaim the acceptable year of the Lord." Luke 4:18-19*

That is Jesus' mission statement. If we are to be the hands of Jesus, the voice of Jesus, the incarnation of the love of Jesus, we too must make it our own.

Our calling is to bring good news to the poor, not to heap more bad news upon them; to proclaim the power of Jesus to release those who are enslaved by their own compulsions rather than to demonise them; to challenge those who are blind to their own wrongdoing, rather than to condemn them; to witness to the power of Jesus to set the oppressed free, rather than to beat them across the head and oppress them further.

For most, learning to love in this way requires a process of healing and growth. Very few emerge from early life without some scars, some hurts, some disappointments. Indeed those who do emerge from childhood unscathed, may have difficulty in coping with the frustrations and difficulties of adult life!

Seeking healing for childhood and teenage hurts, acknowledging and letting go of inferiority and inadequacy, realising that every person in the entire world is a precious person for whom Jesus died are essential steps in the growth of every Christian but above all of every priest.

One cannot truly stand 'in persona Christi' for one's community if one isn't at the very least in the process of dealing with the demons within oneself? It's just not possible. For as long as one attempts to do so, one will be a two-edged sword, cutting both ways, doing good yet spreading hurt, speaking of love yet holding hate.

Unresolved anger, if it is allowed to persist, always has serious repercussions. It becomes an inner poison that flows over into one's relationship. In the case of the priest, it will colour his attitudes and eventually his ministry. He who is called to stand in the person of Christ, called in a special way to incarnate God who is love, will end up incarnating bitterness and resentment. To do that is to be a living tragedy.

Realising that God is love, becoming open to God who is love, entrusting oneself to God who is love, incarnating God who is love is at the heart of the Christian life, and, above all, at the heart of the life of the priest.

God's love, of course, is not a soft love or a love that spoils. It is a love which is prepared to challenge: that is prepared to say, If you would be a disciple of Jesus, this is what you must do. A love that loves the sinner, but then challenges the sinner to stop sinning.

To grow in Christian love, a process of repentance and healing needs to take place in one's own life. One's inner anger and one's selfish tendencies need to be faced, named, acknowledged and then renounced. They are part of what St. Paul describes as our "old self". Jesus died so that we would have the right to be free of our old self.

Victory in Jesus

Ten years ago I came into an insight that has made a big difference in my life, that has indeed enabled me to experience real inner healing and transformation. I came into this insight when reading a commentary on Romans 6:6-12. Through it, I came into a way of praying that enabled me to become open to the power of Jesus to bring ongoing healing into my life. St. Paul says,

"Our old self was crucified with Him so that the sinful body might be destroyed, and we might no longer be enslaved to sin." Romans 6:6

This means that Jesus has won for us the right to be free of our old self. Our victory has already taken place in Jesus. It is there for us in Him. Jesus has won for us the right to be free of our selfish instincts and our compulsions, to have them broken, to set us free.

But coming into that victory involves a process. It goes without saying that, for starters, one should be making every effort to grow in one's relationship with Jesus, to entrust one's life to Him, to become open to the working of the Holy Spirit.

Repentance is also required. One cannot break a habit while indulging it. One must be willing to face the truth about one's inclinations and about the damage that they are doing. This involves acknowledging the existence of the tendency, and seeking to understand where it may have come from or how it may have developed. Sometimes this requires counselling.

Then one must be willing to fast from the compulsion or failing; to abstain from indulging it even when it is not easy to abstain.

"Let not sin therefore reign in your mortal bodies, to make you obey their passions" Romans 6:12.

Jesus asks, "Do you want to be healed?" John 5:6. One does not want to be healed as long as one is indulging one's compulsions. The clearest example of this is with sexuality. The person who has a heap of pornographic material or who goes on watching pornographic films, does not have a real desire to be set free, does not desire to be healed.

So too with anger. As long as one keeps justifying one's outbursts and ignoring the damage that they are causing, then one isn't ready for liberation. Whatever the nature of one's compulsion or negative behaviour, there must be repentance before deliverance can begin.

Finally, having entered into a deep relationship with Jesus, and repented of one's wrongdoing, one seeks to claim the victory which Jesus has already won for us. The good news is that Jesus has indeed won for you the right to be free of your compulsions and negative responses and that He desires to see you set free. The victory is already there in Jesus for the claiming.

The Key Step To Claiming The Victory

"Consider yourselves dead to sin and alive to God in Christ Jesus" Romans 6:11.

Another word for 'consider' is reckon. So it is, "Reckon yourselves dead to sin and alive to God in Christ Jesus."

St. Paul wasn't indulging in religious talk. Through personal experience, Paul had come to know that Jesus had won for us the right to be free of our old selves, that Jesus had taken our old selves with Him to the cross, that, through Jesus' victory, we too could be set free.

Call to mind where you have a wrong tendency. In your mind's eye, invite Jesus into the situation. Then mentally picture yourself being set free by Him. Begin to do this in a systematic way each day and you will enter upon a process of transformation.

I have been using this process for ten years and I have found that it really works. It is using prayer to daily live Paul's instruction, "Reckon yourselves dead to sin and alive to God in Christ Jesus."

During those ten years I used a little hand written notebook, using this process to seek healing. I found it a powerful way to pray, a way that at once brought me very close to Jesus and at the same time brought healing and deliverance into my life.

As well as claiming victory over my 'old self', I included prayer thoughts to help me grow in my relationship with Jesus, in my openness to Him, in my love for Him, plus other intentions.

Then in 1998, after using this method of prayer for about 10 years, I published it in a little prayer booklet, "A Shower of Blessings". I got 10,000 copies printed on the basis that I had the rest of my life in which to sell them. Without publicity, except in the Curate's Diary, the 10,000 sold in the first 10 weeks after publication. We got a further 10,000 printed and they sold in a further 10 weeks. Then we got a further 30,000 printed and they also sold quickly. We have now got a another 30,000 printed. Many have testified that it has helped them to experience inner healing and inner transformation, as well as helping them in prayer.

But the main thing is that, in order to truly become the hands of Jesus, we need to be transformed by Him. In seeking transformation, we are merely seeking what Jesus desires for us. He desires to enable us to truly be transfigured and then we in turn can be His living presence in the world, becoming His hands, His feet, His voice, instruments indeed of His love.

10

The path to Christian inner harmony

When I was growing up, if the Blessed Sacrament was exposed, one made what was called a 'double genuflection"; that is one went down on both knees and bowed. Then, that was changed to a simple genuflection. Now, many just bow.

Our actions represent an attitude, a way of thinking. Genuflection, when properly done, is an act of deep reverence, an acceptance that one is in the presence of God, an act of humility and submission, an acknowledgement that God is God.

Bowing, even solemn bowing, is more a sign of respect. As I see it, one bows to an earthly dignitary, but one genuflects to Jesus Christ. Jesus, one's Lord and God, the one who desires to transform us from within, deserves more than the nod of one's head!

As one grows in one's relationship with Jesus, one desires to find ways of expressing one's love for Him, and of expressing, by one's body actions, total openness to Him, one's desire for total transformation. Genuflecting, then, becomes an expression of what is happening in one's heart.

When one genuflects, one is also fulfilling the Biblical prophecies,

"Therefore God has highly exalted him and bestowed on him the name which is above every name, that at the name of Jesus every knee should bow, in heaven and on earth and under the earth, and every tongue confess that Jesus Christ is Lord, to the glory of God the Father" Philippines 2:9-11.

"As I live, says the Lord, every knee shall bow to me, And every tongue shall give praise to God" (Romans 14:11)

Conscience

Genuflecting, however, isn't popular in today's culture. In so many ways, man is proclaiming himself, if not God's equal, at least His autonomous agent. We see this especially in modern attitudes to conscience and decision making.

So often, the independence of man is stressed; the claim is that God gave us a conscience and free will so that we may make independent decisions. In this view of reality, God is a very distant God who has equipped us with free will, conscience and an intellect and then left us to our own devices. But that isn't the authentic Christian position. Nor was free will given to us so that we could be autonomous. It was given to us so that we could freely decide to love.

Love is not love if it is not freely given. An animal, like say a dog, may be very deeply attached to someone or to another animal. It may be capable of great loyalty and great affection. But it is not capable of making a free decision to love. That is where the human differs from the animal. We can make a decision to love. Even when we don't feel in the mood to love, we can still decide to love, opt for love.

Opting for love involves a degree of surrender. We see this in marriage. Decision making for the person who is living their marriage vows is different to decision making for the bachelor or spinster. In opting for the love relationship of marriage, one has surrendered one's right to independent decision making. What is true of the human relationship of marriage is even more true of our relationship with God. Much more so.

The starting position of authentic Christian living is the acceptance of God as God, the appropriate humility of the created coming before the creator. On top of that, in opting for a love relationship with God, first of all we must accept Jesus as Saviour. Jesus became Saviour when he died for us. But He only becomes MY Saviour when I accept the salvation He has won for me, and accepting salvation involves a real surrender.

It involves the recognition that we are sinners, that we cannot save ourselves, that we must instead surrender ourselves into the salvation that He has won for us. We are called to accept Jesus as both our personal Saviour and as Lord of our lives.

Jesus never said, 'Go, using the conscience and intelligence that I have given you, and make your own decisions.' He said, *"Go therefore and make disciples of all nations, baptizing them in the name of the Father and of the Son and of the Holy Spirit, teaching them to observe all that I have commanded you" Mt. 28:19-20.*

Note how He said, "teaching them to observe all that I have commanded you"! He didn't say, teaching them to follow their consciences or teaching them how to make up their own minds.

But, you may say, didn't Jesus send us the Holy Spirit to help us in our decision making? Yes, but the Bible tells us that the Holy Spirit is God's gift to those who obey Him, (Cf. Acts 5:32).

In Jesus, we are raised up to be His brothers and sisters. But we are only raised up when we have first knelt down. To truly live in Jesus, one must repent of seeking to go one's own way, of seeking to be autonomous.

Father's Plan

When Father created humans, He planned that a truly wonderful relationship would exist between man and God, a relationship that would be a source of great joy and happiness. Somehow man messed up the whole plan and the results of sin became more and more deeply ingrained in man.

Then Father began the rescue mission with Jesus eventually coming to save us. But even after Jesus, the effects of sin are still deeply ingrained in the human condition. Our thinking, our attitudes, our desires, our responses are all contaminated.

Jesus has won for us the right to be free of all this, the right to be delivered, healed and transformed. He is willing to walk with us right back to the moment of our conception. He is willing to penetrate every area of our minds and hearts with His light. He is willing to bring about a truly fabulous change within us, to bring healing where we are hurt, deliverance where we are enslaved, warmth where we are numbed, new life where we experience deadness.

All this is truly wonderful, but it will not happen by chance. We must embrace God's plan. In embracing God's plan we embrace life; in deciding to do our own thing, we embrace death. Do not fool yourself nor let anyone fool you. If you in 'following your conscience', opt for that which is contrary to the teaching of Jesus, you are embracing death. That entire area of your life will be outside God's plan, and while you may still have a relationship with Jesus, there will be little if any further growth in your life.

Living in harmony

We are called to harmony, to experience inner harmony. But we will not experience inner harmony until we are in harmony with God and with God's plan for our lives and for the world. Jesus was in total harmony with His Father.

"I am in the Father and the Father in me" (John 14:10).
"If you had known me, you would have known the Father" (John 14:7).
"He who sees me sees Him who sent me" (John 12:44).

This harmony, this total communion between Jesus and His Father both arose from and led to Jesus doing the will of His Father at all times.

"What I say, therefore, I say as the Father has bidden me" John 12:50.

We are called to share in this harmony between Jesus and His Father.

"If a man loves me, he will keep my word, and my Father will love him, and we will come to him and make our home with him" John 14:23.

Immediately after Jesus said that, He also both promised the Holy Spirit and said, "Peace I leave with you; my peace I give to you." There is an inherent connection between receiving the Holy Spirit, experiencing real inner peace and being in harmony with the teaching of Jesus.

It just isn't possible to be penetrated by the love of Jesus, or to come into a deep ongoing outpouring of the Holy Spirit, or to be filled with the fruits of the Holy Spirit, until there is a conscious decision to do things God's way rather than our own. To the extent that one retains the right to go one's own way, to make one's own independent decisions, one is outside God's plan for one's life.

While this continues, one may have a relationship with Jesus, because regardless of what we do, He still loves us, but one's mind and heart will not be penetrated by His light or by His love, one will not have a deep ongoing experience of the Holy Spirit and the wonderful fruits of the Spirit will be blocked.

I am not speaking theory. I am writing from personal experience. Looking back I can see how I blocked my own progress. I can also see the change that began to occur, when I began to do things God's way, rather than deciding that I knew best, and I see now, that it was only then, that I began to really come under God's anointing and see the blessings flow.

The call to harmony with God's plan for our lives, to repenting of our desire to be independent is also a call to intimacy. Intimacy and harmony go hand in hand.

"He who eats my flesh and drinks my blood abides in me and I in him"
John 6:56.

Eating His flesh and drinking His blood is total communion; it is surrendering ourselves, yielding ourselves to the mind and heart of Jesus; it is becoming one or at-one with Him in His offering of Himself to His Father. That involves being at one with His teaching.

That may appear self-evident, yet many reject elements of the teaching of Jesus. For example, Jesus regularly spoke of the 'evil one', yet many have rejected the concept of satan. Jesus regularly spoke of judgment and of a place of eternal misery, yet many have rejected the concept of hell.

Again Jesus said, "If you love me, you will keep my commandments" (John 14:15), yet many think that their conscience gives them the right to disobey the commandments.

Father is inviting us to truly become His children, to a real relationship with Him, and to live a truly transformed life, but we have to choose.

Footnote - The Role of the Pope

*"And I tell you, you are Peter, and on this rock I will build my Church,
and the powers of death shall not prevail against it. I will give you
the keys of the kingdom of heaven, and whatever you bind on earth
shall be bound in heaven, and whatever you loose on earth shall be
loosed in heaven." Mt. 16:18-20.*

Accepting the teaching of Jesus and of the New Testament includes what
Jesus had to say about the role of Peter. When Jesus used the phrase
"the kingdom of heaven", He was speaking of God's kingdom on earth.
The giving of the keys was very symbolic. In the Old Testament, the
king gave the keys to his prime minister. The one who was given the
keys was the one who was placed in charge. He it was who was given
the authority to bind and to loose, to make rules and to repeal them.

This was the authority that Jesus gave to Peter and implicitly to Peter's
successors. The person who isn't in active communion with Peter and
his successors isn't in communion with God's plan for his Church.

I am not speaking here of infallibility, though that also arises. Neither
am I speaking of an obligation to be in active communion with the Pope
because he is 100% correct on everything. No, what is at issue is being
in active communion with the Pope because he is the Pope. Not because
the Pope is 100% correct on all things, not because he is infallible, but
because he is Pope.

**The person who isn't in active communion with the Pope is at
odds with God's plan for His Church. This applies in the reign of
the present Pope; it applied in the reign of the last Pope and it will
apply in the reign of the next Pope.**

A key element of Jesus' blueprint for the 'kingdom of heaven' here on
earth was that one person should hold the keys, that is, be the effective
prime minister. Within such a system there are ways for working for
change and for seeking to influence opinion that are both positive and
loyal, and there are ways which are divisive, disruptive and damaging.

In seeking to discern which is which, we need only look to politics.
Think what happens when a minister or junior minister or even a
government backbencher starts to publicly attack the prime minister of
the day.

11

Called to be the living presence of Jesus

The word 'incarnation" literally means to embody in flesh, to come in human form. The word 'carnal' means flesh, so "in carnal" means in flesh.

When we speak of the 'Incarnation', we are referring to how the son of God became man. Looked at from the other angle, incarnation is really deification, flesh becoming God. For that is what happened in Jesus. Firstly it was incarnation, God becoming man, but in another sense it was deification, flesh becoming God.

The incarnation of Jesus was a once off event, never to be repeated. But Jesus left us a new form of incarnation,

"He who eats my flesh and drinks my blood, abides in me and I abide in him" John 6:56 .

This is how the mystery of the incarnation is perpetuated: how Jesus makes Himself present to every age and every nation. Incarnation is at the very heart of the Christian faith. Indeed anyone who fails to understand the meaning of incarnation, cannot really begin to understand how God works amongst His people.

During His life on earth, Jesus' power as God was revealed in and through the confines of his human body. He didn't fly around like an angel. He didn't multi-locate or even bilocate.

He did perform miracles which broke the laws of nature as we understand the laws of nature. However that is because we have an essentially secularist understanding of the laws of nature, an understanding of nature that leaves out a most important factor:- the inherent openness of nature to the God who created it.

But essentially Jesus worked from within the human condition, within human limitations. It was from within the human condition that God's love was revealed; one person, Jesus, totally responding to His Father, bringing God's love wherever He went. He, in turn, invited others to also respond to God, to entrust their lives to Him, and to bring God's love wherever they went.

God's love was at no stage poured out independently of incarnation. Whatever happened, including the miracles, was in some way mediated through the human condition. Even where Jesus performed miracles from a distance, they still came about through Him; they didn't just happen separately or independently.

God has chosen to limit Himself to incarnated grace and blessing. He doesn't parachute in to block the Hitlers of this world. He doesn't parachute in to prevent child abuse or any of the other terrible evils. Whatever blessing is brought into the world is in some way mediated through the human condition. We are called to be centres of His love and blessing, to be his hands and feet and voice in today's world.

Before Jesus ascended into heaven, He gave us ways of continuing His presence on earth, the most important of which is the new form of incarnation, an incarnation that comes not through our natural birth but through being born again.. This incarnation is so real that St. Paul could say,

"It is no longer I who live but Christ who lives in me" Galatians 2:20

For the early Church this understanding was the key to Christian living. Through (adult) Baptism, the Christian was immersed in Christ's death and resurrection. In St. Paul the Greek phrase, 'eis Christon', 'into Christ', expresses this immersion of the believer through Baptism and faith. "For as many of you as were baptised into Christ have put on Christ" Galatians 3:27.

Not just immersion indeed, but complete penetration, saturation. Prior to being used as a religious word, the word 'baptism' had two secular meanings - to be flooded with and to be dyed through and through with. Through Baptism and faith the believer is flooded by Jesus, dyed through and through into Him.

When St. Paul speaks of being 'In Jesus' he speaks of a lived experience. It was what he was experiencing in his everyday life. I can truthfully say the same. I do not wish to appear to boast, for I most certainly do not wish to do so. What I am writing here, I write for you. When I speak of how Jesus has touched my life, I do so with a deep humility, realising that I am unworthy, deeply unworthy, that it is all God's work. I share what I am experiencing in the passionate hope that you too might come to experience Jesus as the Bread of your life.

Living In Jesus

"If anyone is in Christ, he is a new creation; the old has passed away, behold the new has come. 2 Corinthians 5:17

St. Paul used a multitude of expressions to try to hammer home how truly the Christian is called to live in Jesus. He used the Greek preposition, 'syn', (with), in several different ways to express this immersion of the believer into Christ. The believer is formed with Jesus, (symmorphos). He is grown together with Jesus (symphytos). He has suffered with Jesus (sympaschein), been crucified with Him (systauroustahai), died with Him (synapothneskein), been buried with Him (synthaptesthai) and been raised with Him (synegeirein).

Again and again he also uses another Greek prep. en, "in", to express how the believer is united with Jesus. "In Christ" occurs a full 165 times in Paul's letters.

Its most common usage expresses the immersion of the Christian into Christ.

"If any one is in Christ, he is a new creature" (2 Cor. 5:17).
"You must consider yourselves dead to sin, but alive to God in Christ Jesus" Romans 6:11.
"There is therefore no condemnation for those who are in Christ Jesus" Romans 8:1.

We are in Christ and Christ is in us.

"Do you not realise that Jesus Christ is in you? - unless indeed you fail to meet the test!" 2 Cor 13:5.

"You are not in the flesh, you are in the Spirit, if the Spirit of God
really dwells within you" Romans 8:9.
"This mystery is .... Christ in you" Col. 1:27.

However, while each true believer is in Christ, it doesn't mean
that there are several million Christs moving around. We are at
once already in Christ and yet we are part of Christ's body.

Coming to live in Jesus and being filled with the Holy Spirit,
has a very positive impact on our inner being, as the joy and
happiness begin to radiate within us,

"All of us, then, reflect the glory of God ...; and that same glory,
coming from the Lord, ... transforms us into His likeness in an ever
greater degree of glory" 2 Cor 3:18, (GN).

How wonderful it is to even begin to experience something of this
glory, something of the love and joy of the Holy Spirit radiating
within us, filling our inner being and beginning to spill over.

Everyone is called to be an 'alter Christus', an 'other Christ'. But
for Christian leaders this is a must!! How can we lead others into
this type of relationship with Jesus, if we are not experiencing it
ourselves? Our leadership role demands that we be the living
presence of Jesus in the world; that we be the hands of Jesus, the
eyes of Jesus, the love of Jesus, having first become His living
tabernacle.

We have no right to expect God to bless our ministry if that is
not so. We may be very enthusiastic, we may be very good
organisers, but if our lives have not been surrendered to Jesus,
transformed by Jesus, then there will be a lack of anointing upon
our work.

Being real about sin

There can never be any form of complacency about personal sin
in the life of any person, much less a priest. While each individual
must at all times be treated with compassion, and while we must
realise that priests do not come ready made, that they have their
own life's journey to face, their own struggles to deal with, yet the
existence of serious personal sin in the life of a priest is a disastrous

situation. Apart from the scandal which it may occasion, God's anointing will be blocked.   The priest, in a very special way, stands in the place of Christ in the Mass. He is the one who is, in the first instance, instructed:- "Do THIS". Every time he ascends to the altar, the priest is called to offer his own life for the people in union with the life, death and resurrection of Jesus.

For this, personal sanctification is a must. If the priest is not incarnating Jesus in his everyday life, in the way he treats people, in his standards, in his personal life, his incarnating of Jesus in the Mass will be gravely deficient.

The priest isn't the only participant in the Mass. He is joined by each member of the faithful. The priest's participation is not nullified if other people present are not walking in Christ, neither is the participation of the faithful nullified if the priest is not living and walking in Christ. But while God in His goodness blesses all who, with sincere hearts, come to Mass regardless of the spiritual and moral condition of others present, much blessing is blocked when the priest either lacks an open heart (enthusiasm) or else has a serious personal problem.

Footnote:- Mass Intentions

This also has important significance for Mass intentions. I once saw a theologian write that the priests own devotion in the Mass was irrelevant to Mass intentions. He is wrong! He has not come to understand the significance of the incarnation, God becoming flesh. The Mass is no more separate to the priest than the Last Supper is separate to Jesus. Without Jesus, no Last Supper; without the priest, no Mass. Who would say that the person and personal disposition of Jesus was irrelevant at the Last Supper?

When the priest offers up intentions during the Mass, he is standing in the place of Jesus. Jesus is the ultimate intercessor, continuously making intercession for us before God the Father. Our intercession has value only through union with Him, through our becoming an extension of His intercession; through allowing His Spirit to intercede within us.

Mass intentions do NOT have a separate value in themselves. They derive their value from the intercession of the person making the offering and then from the intercession of the priest while celebrating Mass; that is while the priest is uniting himself with the self-offering of Jesus to His Father.

Some feel that they can toss in dozens of intercessions during the Mass with the same effectiveness as focusing especially on one or two intercessions. The Mass indeed contains many intercessions which, in union with Jesus, we bring before God the Father. It is also possible for us to include several other intentions, but it is hard to focus on more than one or two.

The argument of those who feel that one can toss in dozens of intentions is that God is all powerful:- one or a dozen makes no difference to Him. They point to the sun's ability to tan millions of people at the one moment.

That it can is true, but there is one thing that the sun would have great difficulty doing:- tanning someone on the back and the front at the same time. The difficulty lies not with the sun, but with us. We can only lie on one side at a time! So too with Mass intentions.

God is all powerful, but the way He works is through incarnation. The blessings that come through the Mass come through the priest and people being united with Jesus' offering of Himself to Father. They come through our entering into this offering of Jesus, through our becoming united with it, and through our living of it in the Mass.

God can instantaneously reach out to millions of people bringing different intentions, but we, as we seek to incarnate Jesus, are working within the limitations of our humanity. As we unite ourselves with the ongoing intercession being made by Jesus we have only the capacity to focus on a small number of intentions at a time.

In this, as in everything else, our calling is to be deeply united with Jesus, to not just bring the intention ourselves, but to unite ourselves with the indwelling Jesus bringing this intention to Father, uniting it with Jesus' total giving of Himself to His Father in intercession for us.

12

Being filled with Love

I no longer depend on human relationships to figure out what God's love is like, nor have I so depended at any stage for the last 27 years. I know what God's love is like because I have an intense ongoing experience of it.

Twenty seven years ago, when I was in the depths of despair, when I was filled with intense emptiness, Jesus became for me the life-giving water that wells up within so that one does not thirst again. For the past 27 years, I have experienced His love at a level deeper than any human person could ever reach.

I was a slow learner, slow to respond to the wonderful gift that Jesus was giving me. I continued to stumble around in the darkness for many years, the darkness created by my own undealt-with anger, the darkness created by my sexual struggles, and the darkness of my own self-seeking and wrong attitudes. Jesus was filling the core of my being with love, yet important parts of my inner self were still beyond his Lordship. This greatly slowed my growth and left me a divided person.

Thankfully with time, I began to respond to His wonderful love, began to recognise the need to deal with the hurt and anger, began to come into sexual healing, began to let go of my need to prove myself, began to allow myself to be transformed. The more progress I made, the more progress became possible, and also the more my openness to the great love of Jesus increased.

It is His will that our experience of His love for us would just grow and grow. This does not happen automatically. We need to really respond. Jesus told the parable of the hidden treasure which when one finds, one leaves everything else aside so as to obtain that treasure.

"The kingdom of heaven is like treasure hidden in a field, which a

man found and covered up; then in his joy he goes and sells all that he
has and buys that field.
"Again, the kingdom of heaven is like a merchant in search of fine
pearls, who, on finding one pearl of great value, went and sold all that
he had and bought it." Matthew 13:44-45

Jesus' love is that treasure. First one finds it. But having found it, becoming open to it and growing in it requires single mindedness. It needs to become the most important reality in one's life. Nothing must be allowed to stand in the way. First one needs to be prepared to seek it until it is found.

People read about Jesus being the Bread of Life, they read about Jesus giving the water that wells up within, but they fail to understand. It just passes over their heads, for them it is just more religious cliches, empty metaphors. Though having eyes, they do not see.

It saddens me when I hear Christian adults, who are still dependent on images derived from human love, as they seek to understand God's love. That isn't the way it is meant to be. Not merely am I not dependent on human love to understand God's love, but the very opposite:- my understanding of human love, and of the type of love to which humans are called, springs from my experience of God's love. That is how I experience it.

That is also how St. Paul experienced it. That is why St. Paul could compare the type of love, which a married couple should have for one another, to Jesus' love for the Church. He was speaking out of his own personal experience of Jesus' love.

St. Paul's ongoing experience of God's love was so real, so deep, that instead of using human relationships to understand God's love for us, he used God's love to help us to understand what we are called to in human relationships. Furthermore he was obviously confident that his readers had a similar experience of God's love, that they too had such a deep experience of God's love, that they would understand how marital love was meant to reflect God's tremendous love for us.

We are all called to this deep experience of God's love, to experience the living water.

"Whoever drinks of the water that I shall give him will never thirst (again); the water that I shall give him will become in him a spring of water welling up to eternal life" John 4:14.

Jesus desires you to be literally filled with His love, for you to have an experience of His love welling up within you. When one comes into that experience, one sees the whole of reality, including human love, in a new light.

From despair to joy

There is in each person a special spiritual centre with a capacity for receiving God's love. This spiritual centre is the same centre with which we experience a sense of awe when beholding beautiful scenery. It can be a great help when one identifies where one's spiritual centre is, because it can enable one to focus more directly on it and on becoming open to the wonderful blessings that are meant to flow through it.

When one's spiritual centre is empty it gets hungry, possibly even very hungry, and one may experience this hunger as a sense of emptiness or of something missing in one's life. In my case, the sense of emptiness was so great that it felt as if there was vacuum inside my chest sucking me in.

Jesus is the Bread of Life who can remove that emptiness, that hunger. One's inner spiritual centre can be filled with a tremendous experience of His love. Later, it is also through one's spiritual centre that the fruit of the Spirit is received, including joy.

Today there are times when I experience such great joy in my spiritual centre that it causes physical pain. My spiritual centre is just not able to cope with the level of joy I experience through the outpouring of the Holy Spirit.

But that is not where most begin in life. It is not normal to start from a position of deep spiritual experience. I didn't. Before I experienced God's love, I went through years of anguish, emptiness. I was attracted by God, I longed to serve God, but I had not experienced Jesus as the life-giving water welling up within. I had not found the hidden treasure.

Today I know what Jesus meant when He spoke of the life giving water welling up within because I have a deep experience of it. I have experienced and continue to experience Jesus as the Bread of Life. I have experienced and continue to experience His love immersing my inner being and my love for Him welling up within me. That is how it is meant to be. It is God's will that every Christian experience Jesus as the Bread of Life.

Jesus never said, love me as you love one another. No! He said, *"Love one another as I have loved you" John 15:12.*
Our capacity to love one another is to spring from our experience of His love. This presumes that we have a real transforming experience of His love.

If one has truly come to know God, one will have such an experience of love and of being filled with love, that it is inconceivable that one will not desire to love. One's capacity for love may yet be imperfect, there may still be matters to be faced and dealt with, but yet there will be an enthusiasm for love.

"He who does not love does not know God" I John 4:8.

Jesus desires to become for you the Bread of Life. He desires you to have a most intense experience of His love. He desires for His love to become more real than any human love could possibly be. For the celibate in particular, there is the call to so experience God's love, that no human love could be as intense, as real, as fulfilling. God wills that the gap created by one's celibacy be filled beyond measure with an intense experience of the indwelling Jesus.

He wills that the person who is called to stand in the shoes of Jesus should be intensely filled with the love of Jesus; that those who seek to incarnate Jesus be filled with the presence of Jesus, transfigured by His love.

Yet this experience of God's love is for all Everybody needs it and both the Church and the world badly need people who have experienced it.

13

"You shall be My Family"

Jesus has truly been my best Friend for over a quarter of a century. My whole life is centred on Him, my spirit expands with a sense of His love, yet I am only gradually beginning to realise how truly Father loves me. Indeed it was only recently I realised that I always called my heavenly Father, "the Father". Now I wouldn't refer to my earthly mother as 'the mother' or my earthly father as 'the father'. It isn't the way one speaks, if one is close to one's parents. One refers to them as 'Mother' and 'Father'. Thus it is "Mother asked me to .." and not "the mother asked me to.."

So too it should be in our relationship with our heavenly Father! Jesus invites us to the level of relationship where we feel free to call Him 'Father' and not 'the Father', the level of relationship where He truly becomes Father to us.

"Those who are led by God's Spirit are God's sons. ... The Spirit makes you God's children, and by the Spirit's power we cry out to God, 'Father! my Father.'" Romans 8:14, 15B, (GN).

Begin to do that and you will see the difference. Slowly repeat 'Father' to yourself, fixing your gaze on Him. Father will begin to become a very real person for you. Right now He desires to meet you in a new way. Father loves you and He wants you to know it.

He loves each of us with an infinite love and we don't begin to realise it. Part of the reason we don't realise it, is that we haven't been told. The reason we haven't been told, is that it is not part of the lived experience of our people.

Again, part of the problem is that we have turned the sacraments into mere rituals. If Baptism was being properly confirmed and renewed, every genuine Christian would have a deep experience of Father's love, just as on the occasion of His Baptism, Jesus heard Father's voice declaring,

"This is my beloved son with whom I am well pleased" Mt. 3:17.

We have been cheated out of our inheritance, out of the great
blessings that Father has for us, the experience of being loved by
Him, the experience of knowing that we are special in His eyes,
the experience of knowing Him as Father. Jesus desires to draw
us into real intimacy with Father, desires that we know our dignity
as members of Father's family, desires that we too would hear
Father's voice saying,

"You are precious in my eyes and honoured and I love you" Isaiah 43:4.

There is however a second reason why one may not be
experiencing Father's love. One may not be open to listening to
His voice. The prodigal son was loved by his father even while he
was ruining his own life, but he had turned his back on that love.
Before he could hear his father's voice, he had to come to his senses,
and admit his own unworthiness. As long as he kept ruining his
life, his inner ear was completely deaf. His father still loved him,
but that was of no use to the son whatsoever.

I too had to come to my senses. Father loved me all the time.
Indeed He knew that I would eventually respond, that my ears
would eventually be opened to hear His voice, but until I faced my
own inner demons, there was a cloud of my own making preventing
the true sun, Father's love, from enveloping me.

It was like sitting on the beach on a broken day, sometimes the
sun would break through, then the clouds would come, then the
rain, then the sun again. It was a long slow process. Only today,
27 years after Jesus truly became the Bread of Life for me, am I
beginning to truly experience what it is to be loved by Father.

God told His people,

"Obey my voice and I will be your God and you shall be my people;
and walk in all the ways that I shall command you, that it may be well
with you" Jeremiah 7:23.

The Hebrew word for "people" is also the word for 'family'. So
God is telling them "You shall be my family and I will be your
God." But to experience the love of Father, they had to listen to
His voice and be guided by Him.

Father invites us to be His family. He loves us deeply. He
loves us unconditionally. He loves us with an infinite love.

However, again and again we see that when people fail to respond to Father's love, it has consequences. Father desires to bless us in many ways, but these blessings can only flow when one responds to His love. Until one responds, the door to one's heart remains closed, and nobody except oneself can open it. Father loves us, but He is not a burglar. He will not break in, He will not prise the door open. Thus it is,

"Obey my voice and I will be your God and you shall be my people; and walk in all the ways that I shall command you, that it may be well with you" Jeremiah 7:23.

Until we obey His voice, He is still God, but He is not OUR God! He may be 'the Father' but He is not 'Father'. If we are not obeying His voice, then we are obeying some other voice. Something else or someone else is our God. He desires to bless us, but until we learn to seek to live a love centred life, the blessings cannot flow.

I once heard the story of an impatient farmer, who lived back in the old days, when calves were still fed out of buckets. When he brought the calves their feed, if they didn't drink it up quickly, he would throw it over them saying, "If you won't have it one way, you can have it the other."

Father isn't like that! He will seek us out, spend time with us, pursue us, but He will not throw the blessings over us. We can only receive them by drinking, that is by opening our hearts to Him and to the wonderful way in which He invites us to live. **Right now He is waiting for you. He is ready whenever you are.**

The prophets were filled with a sense of Father's love for His people. It is clear that they themselves enjoyed a relationship of remarkable intimacy with Him. He truly was their God and they knew what it was to be His family.

The Prophet Hosea

"I will betroth you to Me for ever: I will betroth you to me in righteousness and in justice, in steadfast love, and in mercy, I will betroth you to Me in faithfulness: and you shall know the Lord" Hosea 2:19-20.

Hosea presents powerful images of God as the loving Husband and of His great love and faithfulness in the face of great unfaithfulness by His bride, the people.

"She shall pursue her lovers, but not overtake them:
and she shall seek them, but shall not find them.
Then she shall say, 'I will go and return to my first husband,
for it was better with me then than now.
And she did not know that it was I who gave her the grain,
the wine, and the oil, and who lavished upon her silver
and gold which they used for Ba'al" Hosea 2:7-8.

"Therefore, behold, I will allure her,
and bring her into the wilderness,
and speak tenderly to her.
And there I will give her vineyards,
and make the Valley of Anchor a door of hope.
And there she shall answer as in the days of her youth,
as at the time when she came out of the land of Egypt" Hosea 2:14-15.

The Prophet Isaiah

"For your Maker is your husband, the Lord of hosts is his name; and the Holy One of Israel is your Redeemer, the God of the whole earth, He is called. For the Lord has called you like a wife forsaken and grieved in spirit, like a wife of youth when she is cast off, says your God. For a brief moment I forsook you, but with great compassion I will gather you. In overflowing wrath for a moment I hid my face from you, but with everlasting love I will have compassion on you, says the Lord, your Redeemer." Isaiah 54:5-8.

"For the Lord delights in you, and your land shall be married."
Isaiah 62:4f.

The Prophet Jeremiah

"Thus says the Lord, 'I remember the devotion of your youth, your love as a bride'" Jeremiah 2:2.
"Surely, as a faithless wife leaves her husband, so you have been faithless to me, O house of Israel, says the Lord." Jeremiah 3:20.

The Prophet Ezekiel

The prophet Ezekiel even accuses the people of adultery for failing to be faithful to God:-

"Adulterous wife who receives strangers instead of her husband"
Ezekiel 16:32.
"Declare to them their abominable deeds. For they have committed
adultery." Ezekiel 23:36.

The Song of Solomon

The highest Old Testament expression of the husband - wife relationship between God and His people is to be found in the "Song of Solomon" (the Canticle of Canticles.) In it a series of love songs are used to express God's infinite love for us.

"Behold, you are beautiful, my love:
behold you are beautiful:
your eyes are doves.
Behold you are beautiful, my beloved,
truly lovely. (Song of Solomon 1:15 - 16)

This understanding of God's tremendous love, of the way in which He draws His people to Himself, of it being a real covenant like a marriage covenant leaps off the pages of the Old Testament. Only people who were themselves having an intense experience of Father's love could write in this way.

Footnote:- Jesus is the bridegroom

Jesus reveals that the one God is really a family. The first person of this family is revealed to us as Abba, Dad, Father. Jesus desires that you and I would come to Father with the same confidence that a child would approach its daddy.

Jesus remained celibate. He loved the people with an exclusive love, a total love, an all-giving love. There was no room for a wife in His life, because He gave Himself totally and completely to all and for all. As the Bible tells us, He "had but one bride, the Church." Taking the people as His bride, and seeking to enable them to grow in this spousal relationship, there was no room for another bride. His relationship with all was such that He could not belong exclusively to one.

John the Baptist announces Jesus as the bridegroom.

"The friend of the bridegroom, who stands and hears Him, rejoices
greatly at the bridegroom's voice: therefore this joy of mine is now
full" John 3:29

Jesus also saw Himself as the bridegroom.

"Can the wedding guests fast while the bridegroom is with them? As long as they have the bridegroom with them, they cannot fast. The days will come, when the bridegroom is taken away from them, and then they will fast in that day." Mark 2:19-20.

St. Paul declares,

"I feel a divine jealousy for you, because I gave you in marriage to
one husband to present you as a pure virgin to Christ"
2 Corinthians 11:2 (paraphrased).

Meanwhile, such is the extent of clarity, with which the people understood Jesus' role in terms of taking the people as His bride, that in Ephesians St. Paul presents Jesus' love for the Church as the real marriage. Human marriage finds its dignity in being an image of this. Thus He can say,

"Husbands, love your wives, even as Christ loved the Church and
gave Himself up for her" Eph. 5:25.

St. Paul describes this intimate relationship between Jesus and the Church as part of the "great mystery" of salvation. In the Book of Revelation, Jesus is again presented as the bridegroom.

"Let us rejoice and exult and give him the glory.
For the marriage of the Lamb has come,
and his Bride has made herself ready;
it was granted her to be clothed with fine linen, bright and pure,
for the fine linen is the righteous deeds of the saints.
And the angel said to me, 'Write this:
Blessed are those who are invited to the marriage supper of the
Lamb." (Revelation 19:7-9).

"And I saw the holy city, the new Jerusalem, coming down out of
heaven from God, prepared as a bride adorned for her husband"
(Revelation 21:2).

A Strong Argument

A theologian, who opposes celibacy, recently said, "The only argument for celibacy is that Jesus was celibate." How close to the truth he is! Once one understands the full meaning and significance of the celibacy of Jesus, the arguments for either priestly celibacy or, if married men are ordained, for priestly continence become very powerful, for the priest is called to be deeply united with Jesus, the Bridegroom, to be the best man who leaves his own family to wait upon the Groom.

14

Becoming God's Family

"Here are my mother and my brethren! Whoever does the will of God is my brother, and sister, and mother" Mark 3:34.

Jesus said this on the occasion when He was told that his mother and relatives were "standing outside". People have been so distracted by the question of whether He was snubbing His mother, which He wasn't, that they fail to see what He was really saying, namely, that He was creating a new family, and that his followers were to learn to treat each other as family.

Jesus often said things in a very dramatic way, said things in a way designed to wake up his listeners, to even shock them as He strove to open their minds and hearts to new ideas. This was one such occasion. He really desired that His followers would see one another as family, would learn to be family together, but people then were as individualistic and divided as they are today. They often heard what He said, yet hadn't ears to hear. In other words, they heard, but it didn't register.

In the Old Testament, God had invited the people to be His family. When they obeyed His voice, He became their God and they His family. Here Jesus, as God, made the message as direct and as personal as He possibly could. "Here are my mother and my brethren! Whoever does the will of God is my brother, and sister, and mother."

If we are to truly share in the ministry of Jesus, we too must learn to do the same. Just as Sylvia Lubich and her young friends looked into each other's eyes and declared, "I am willing to lay down my life for you," we must look into each other's eyes and, in our spirits, declare "You are my family."

Become conscious of the people around you on a Sunday morning in church, and, in your spirit, declare, "This is my family." Allow yourself to take it in, to truly realise it, that all the people around you at Mass are in a very real sense your family, and, as family, you are called to enter a special bond with them.

Having started to do so at Mass, begin to do so at every parish function you attend. Look around you, see the other parishioners there and within yourself repeat, "This is my family." Allow yourself to develop a bond of affection for every person. Begin to move away from being just a committed parishioner to being a committed family member. The difference is the bond that one is called to create with each person. It will, in turn, create a difference in the way you relate to people and the way you mix among them. If you see someone as your brother or sister, you will desire to speak to them, to encourage them and to be there for them.

This is something that I have only gradually learned. When I was ordained first, though I was very enthusiastic, I saw the people as 'them' not as family. I saw it as my calling to preach to 'them', to convert 'them', to challenge 'them', to even love 'them'. I didn't realise that I was called to create family bonds, called to be able to say with Jesus, "Here are my mother and my brethren! Whoever does the will of God is my brother, and sister, and mother."

The transition takes time. First one needs to discover that this is the plan of Jesus. Then one has to learn to put this insight into practice; to learn to see and treat each person as one's brother, sister, mother.

Father's plan is to create a family spirit, to enable us to turn our parishes into real family communities. This doesn't mean living out of each other's pockets or taking away one another's privacy. It involves rather a whole new attitude of caring for one another, of being willing to let go of past differences and hurts, of being willing to welcome newcomers, of being willing to reintegrate those who have cut themselves off, of being there to encourage those who may be embarrassed by family circumstances, and of being willing to love in an unconditional and non-judgemental way.

Whatever other family members do, whatever mistakes they make, our calling is to love them. If we truly love them, we will pray for them, we may even challenge them, but we won't judge them.

The Priest's Role In Creating Family

The priest isn't just a functionary. He isn't just doing a job, not even a very special job. There are many dedicated professions, many caring professions. But there is ONLY one in which the person is called to daily mount the altar and declare, "I am giving my life for you"; only one in which the person is called to renounce the possibility of belonging exclusively to one person so that he can give himself for all.

Some think that because Jesus took the people as His bride, that the priest is meant to take the people as bride also. He isn't! There is but one Bridegroom, because there is but one Bread of Life, and that is Jesus. The priest cannot be the people's spouse because he is not their Bread of Life. His role is that of the best man - except that it is a lifelong role rather than a one day stand. As best man, he is called to attend upon the Groom, to speak for the Groom, to introduce people to the Groom and, on the Groom's behalf, to build a family spirit. He is called to stand in the place of the Groom, yet he is but a signpost pointing to the Groom. The only place any person can experience Jesus is in their spiritual centre, and that centre is accessible only to Jesus and the Holy Spirit.

For the authentic living of his celibate calling, the priest must be a builder of family bonds, fostering community, drawing people into a special relationship with one another and with himself.

Some priests have a fantastic gift for drawing people to themselves, but they do so for the wrong reasons. The man who is continuously running around, seeking to stand on his head for everybody, may be doing so out of a terrible need for love and approval. Deep down, he may be terribly lonely, and may have an insatiable compulsion to have people approve both of him and of what he is doing. Such a priest may be the most popular man around, the people may love him, but depending on the extent of his needs, he may be a walking tragedy.

For the first five to ten years of his ministry, it would be totally normal for the need for recognition to be of significant importance to a priest. It should, however, be of diminishing importance! If one has a craving for recognition, one is in trouble. One will be forever doing things to seek approval, to win acclaim, to be popular and no matter how much approval one gets, it will not satisfy one's need.

Sadly, such a priest may also be vulnerable sexually - through no fault of his own, it being a given handicap. Our sexuality is a very important area of our personality, and it is interconnected with all the other important areas. One cannot put one's sexuality into a separate compartment. If one is hurt in the area of sexuality, it will impact on other key areas. If one is hurt in a way that leaves one requiring extra love and approval, it could impact greatly on one's sexuality. This applies to everyone.

For such a person, unless he comes into real healing, the practical living of celibacy, in its demand for complete continence, will be at best extremely difficult, and perhaps impossible. Impossible, that is, until one finds Jesus as the Bread of Life, until one begins to experience the life-giving water welling up within, until one begins to be touched and healed by Jesus.

"For with God nothing will be impossible" Luke 1:37.

In some ways one can learn from the person with the compulsive need for approval, because he will often be an expert at making himself loved. Self and his own needs may dominate, yet we can learn from the way he reaches out to people. In his need, he does some of the things for self-centred reasons which we should all be doing for the sake of the kingdom. For he is continuously reaching out to people and inviting them into a relationship. He does so out of his own inner craving; we, however, need to invite people into a love relationship that isn't self-seeking; one that is quite the opposite, that springs from our desire to introduce people to a living relationship with Jesus and then to become family together.

Come and See

"Jesus turned, saw them following him, and asked, 'What are you looking for?' They answered 'Where do you live, Rabbi?' 'Come and see', he answered. So they went with him, and saw where he lived and spent the rest of that day with him." John 1:37-39 (GN)

It was after Andrew and his friend had spent the evening with Jesus, that Andrew was able to go to his brother, Simon Peter and say,

"We have found the Messiah" (John 1:41)

It wasn't in the first place because of His teaching nor even because of His working miracles, but because Jesus shared His life with them for that evening, that they came to recognise that He was the Messiah, and with this knowledge, they were then able to go to their families to invite them also to 'Come and see'.

We too must be giving the people this invitation:- Come and see. We have to let down barriers, and like Jesus, invite people to share our lives, to see where we live and, above all, to see the joy and hope that fills our lives. We have something to share, and we are called to share it.

The wonderful thing about being a Jesus-filled Christian is that the more you give, the more you get. You never lose by sharing Jesus with others. Quite the contrary, for in seeking to share something of the love of Jesus with others, one allows the Holy Spirit to work within oneself. If Jesus is truly in one's life, the more one seeks to share this with others, the more full of the Holy Spirit one becomes.

Every Christian is called to lead people to Jesus, and to draw them into community, but for the priest, it should be a central part of his ministry. Just as marriage cannot be lived by a person who insists on cutting himself off from his bride, never lets her know where he is going or what he is doing, neither can celibacy be lived by a priest who insists on cutting himself off from his people. He may be continent, just as the husband may be faithful sexually, but he is not living priestly celibacy.

There must be self-revelation. He must share himself as He seeks to share Jesus with them. He must learn to let down barriers and let the people see who he is.

That docsn't mean that one cannot have one's own private space. Jesus didn't allow people to manipulate Him or to take Him over. *"Very early the next morning, long before daylight, Jesus got up and left the house. He went out of the town to a lonely place, where he prayed. But Simon and his companions went out searching for him, and when they found him, they said, 'Everyone is looking for you.' But Jesus answered, 'We must go on to the other villages round here. I have to preach in them also, because that is why I came." Mark 1:35 - 38 (GN)*

There was the ongoing balance: 'Come and see", was balanced by His taking time to be alone, by His even hiding when the people desired to manipulate Him. Yet the primary thrust of his mission was, "Come and see":- an ongoing invitation to the people to share in His life; to understand both who he was and His mission.

This same thrust must energise the ministry of the priest. In living out His celibate calling, he invites the people to enter into a special relationship with himself and, through him, with Jesus. This involves inviting the people, especially those who have become disciples or who are potential disciples, to enter behind the barriers, to come to see and know him for who he is, both as a person and as a priest; to come too to understand the nature of his celibate calling.

This is indeed the very heart of celibacy. I, as a priest, have given up the right to marry, not to live in splendid isolation, not to live as a gentleman bachelor, but rather to enter into a special relationship with the people entrusted to my care; to share something of the love of Jesus with them; to look into their eyes and declare, "Here are my mother and my brethren! Whoever does the will of God is my brother, and sister, and mother".

Then, in return, I invite the people to become family together, with Jesus at the centre. I, as priest, can only give the invitation. It is an invitation that calls for a response.

15

The Single Person's Source Of Inner Nourishment

Receiving One's Daily Bread

The priest, as best man, invites the people into a family relationship. But from where does he draw the strength for this relationship, the ongoing nourishment that he himself needs for his own fulfilment and well being? Likewise from where does the dedicated single person, the widow(er) and the separated person draw their strength?

The married man draws much of his personal nourishment and fulfilment from his relationship with his wife. Though it must be said that single people, including priests, tend to have a very romanticised perception of marriage - a perception that takes little account of all the practical situations that do arise:- long-term illness, psychiatric problems, difficulties in communication, financial, work and family pressures, not to speak of betrayal and unfaithfulness.

Many is the married person who is being called to live the authentic Christian life while drawing very little, if any, sustenance from his or her spouse and yet having to shoulder all the responsibilities of family life. However, in theory at least, and thankfully very often in practice, married people receive real strength and fulfilment from their relationship with their spouse.

There are those who say that the priest should find it from his love relationship with his people; from growing in the ability to love and to allow himself to be loved. They develop this understanding because they believe, wrongly, that the priest is called to take the people as his bride.

Those who see it this way, have made a very important contribution, for they focus on the importance of the priest developing a real relationship with his people; on his learning to let down the shutters and to allow himself to be known as a real person; on his drawing the people into a degree of intimacy with himself as he seeks to stand in the place of Christ (in persona Christi) for them.

But the priest is not the Bridegroom. Indeed he can no more be the Bridegroom than he can be the Bread of Life. There is but one Bridegroom, Jesus. The priest's role is that of best man.

Further, the priest who believes that he is to draw his most basic sustenance from his people is seeking it in a place where it isn't to be found. This too has dangers.

No, both the priest and the single person must find an even extra degree of sustenance from their relationship with Jesus Himself. They are called to an even deeper experience of Jesus as the Bread of Life. Whatever emptiness there is in their lives, should become the openness to an even more intense relationship with Jesus. From my own personal experience, I know that the gap can be filled by Jesus. Jesus has led me to a level of relationship with Himself that is truly fabulous, way beyond what I thought possible.

In a sense, to be single is an advantage. If one is married, one never knows when one will lose one's spouse and then one is left with a major gap, possibly suddenly. If one is single, one should, all the time, be putting all one's energy into growing in one's relationship with Jesus, experiencing the outpouring of the Holy Spirit and of Father's love.

Whatever it takes

If you don't know Jesus in this way, if He isn't yet the Bread of Life for you, if you don't experience Him as your very best Friend, then drop everything and go seek Him. Don't stop seeking, until you can truly say, that you experience Jesus as your Bread of Life. It is not enough for you to acknowledge Jesus as the Bread of Life. He must become your Bread of Life. Jesus is saying to you,

"Ask, and it will be given you; seek, and you will find; knock, and it will be opened to you. For everyone who asks receives, and he who

seeks finds, and to him who knocks it will be opened." Luke 11:9-10
Jesus speaks in this passage about receiving the Holy Spirit. The passage goes on to stress the enthusiasm of Father to give us the Holy Spirit.
"How much more will the heavenly Father give the Holy Spirit to those who ask him" Luke 11:13.
But, one can only truly receive the Holy Spirit once Jesus has become one's Bread of Life. Receiving Jesus as the Bread of Life is the first step. So the passage about asking and receiving can be applied also to receiving Jesus. And a more correct translation from the original Greek would read, Go on asking, Go on seeking, Go on knocking. The asking, seeking, knocking needs to be continuous, ongoing.

The most important undertaking open to a person is to come to really know Jesus as the Bread of Life, as the life-giving water welling up within. I know how I came into that experience and I have shared it with you. Each person is unique. I don't know how you are meant to encounter Jesus, but I do know that it is God's will for you. All I can say is, go on asking, seeking, knocking, until you truly know that Jesus is living within you.

It is seldom that it happens in isolation. Seek Jesus where He is to be found. Seek Him in the company of those who have found Him, because they are in the best position to help you to find Him also. They know what it is to have Jesus as their best Friend. Having experienced it themselves, their prayers and their witness will be far more effective.

Then, once Jesus becomes your best Friend, be generous in spending time with Him. No friendship can grow without quality time. No friendship can grow if one party gives time to it only when it feels good, or when it suits them. Jesus desires that you spend a certain length of time with Him in prayer each day. Get the Holy Spirit to show you what length of time you are called to spend with Jesus, then be loyal to it. If you expect to be happy in His presence for eternity in heaven, get used to spending quality time with Him each day. Mind, I do not tell you to spend time ᵧ ..₁g prayers, but, rather, to spend time in prayer. There is an enormous difference. One can say many prayers yet not be touched by them. This is one of the great weaknesses in our Catholic tradition. Far too often we keep our prayers in a separate compartment. We say our prayers, even go to Mass, and then continue on the same as ever. That isn't Christian prayer.

Christian prayer is about spending time with Jesus, about allowing ourselves to be filled with His presence and with love for Him. It is about rebirth, transformation, being changed from within; about opening our lives to His transforming power, becoming open to the wonderful victory that He has won for us.

Prayer also needs nourishment. Each year I spend almost a week on a holy holiday in Knock, and another 4 to 5 days at the Intercession for Priests. Most years I also go on a pilgrimage, and I attend a conference or two. Add in spiritual reading and listening to tapes. All this helps. It provides the atmosphere and opportunity for growth. Sometimes it may be the occasion of special blessing.

For the priest and the dedicated single person, all this is so important. There is no other viable alternative. Either one finds the inner sustenance for celibate living in one's relationship with Jesus, or one doesn't find it.

There may be many other supports in one's life - family, friends, colleagues, a growing relationship with the people. These are all very important, indeed essential, but there is only one source from which one can draw the most basic sustenance of all, and that is Jesus Himself.

If one is receiving adequate ongoing sustenance from one's relationship with Jesus, then all one's other relationships take on special value, and one is in a position to appreciate them and to be enriched by them. But if one isn't receiving adequate sustenance from one's relationship with Jesus, then there will be a serious ongoing gap in one's inner life.

Not merely will there be a big gap, but it is a gap that makes demands. One will experience it as a gap, as a compelling need, as a form of incompleteness or loneliness, and consciously or unconsciously, one will experience temptation to find a substitute - perhaps through a relationship, perhaps through drink, perhaps through nonstop activity.

This is indeed true of everyone. There is an inner emptiness within the human person which can only ultimately be satisfied by a deep relationship with Jesus. It is from this deep spiritual relationship, that one is meant to find the strength to face the vicissitudes of life, including the vicissitudes of married life.

The woman with five husbands

Jesus once met a woman who obviously had deep inner needs, and who had sought to satisfy these inner needs through relationships. She had had five husbands, but the man with whom she was then living was not her husband.

It was to this extremely needy person, this lady whose inner needs caused her to crave love and affection, that Jesus made one of His most important promises.

"Whoever drinks of the water that I shall give him will never thirst; the water that I shall give him will become in him a spring of water welling up to eternal life" John 4:14.

Jesus also promised,

"I am the bread of life; he who comes to me shall not hunger, and he who believes in me shall never thirst" John 6:35.

These promises are for everyone, married and single. But the dedicated single person is called to truly live them and to live by them. Jesus must become for him the anchor of his life, his very foundation, his source of sustenance, the Bread of Life, the Life-giving water.

The dedicated single person's very life must become an incarnated witness that Jesus is the Bread of Life, that Jesus does provide water that quenches the inner emotional thirst. The goal of the single person's spiritual journey should be to be able to say with St. Paul,

"It is no longer I who live, but Christ who lives in me."

This however does not happen by accident, nor does it happen overnight. There may be special moments of blessing, just as there are in the marriage relationship, but just as, regardless of honeymoon experiences, the marriage relationship needs commitment, needs to be worked at, so too does our relationship with Jesus. As Jesus said,

"Go on asking and it will be given to you; go on seeking and you will
   find; go on knocking, and the door will be opened to you. For
   everyone who goes on asking, receives, and the one who goes on
   seeking, finds, and the one who keeps knocking has the door opened.
... Of course the heavenly Father will give the Holy Spirit to those who
   keep asking Him!" Luke 11:9-10, 13 (My wording)

Growth is necessary

The asking, seeking, knocking needs to be continuous, ongoing. Not because of any reluctance on the part of Jesus, but rather because of the limitations of the human condition! Through our past wrong choices, we have built up a resistance to God's anointing. Part of us desires to become open to the full outpouring of the Holy Spirit while another part of our inner selves still resists.

The fastest way to let fresh air into a bottle full of dirty water is to first get rid of the dirty water. With a bottle it is quite easy, but with our inner selves, especially if they have become badly mucked up, the cleansing can take a long time. We need a transformation that involves allowing the light and love of Jesus to penetrate every memory, every thought, every attitude.

Then there is the growth factor. Growth is an inherent dimension of being human. Part of our God given design is to grow, to develop. There is a beginning and then there is gradual growth. This applies to our relationship with Jesus and to our openness to the Holy Spirit. We are designed to grow, to continue to develop an ever deeper relationship, to become more and more open.

It is wonderful to be able to say, "Yes", today to Jesus and to His plan for one's life, but tomorrow we will need to say a new, "Yes", a "Yes", that is a further step forward, that reflects the person that we have now become, that reflects further willingness for growth in our relationship with Jesus.

Living, being human, is centred on growth and development. In the physical body, this growth and development is largely limited to the first third of the human life-span. But not so within the spiritual or even the emotional dimensions of our being. Here the call is to go on growing and growing; to go on growing and growing in our capacity for loving, and to go on growing and growing in our relationship and intimacy with God.

If our relationship with God is to be a growing one, then that means it doesn't happen all at once. There is a beginning and there is growth. Seldom will this growth be visible to the human eye, no more than is the growth of the grass or the growth of our hair.

They are growing all the time, or at least whenever conditions are right, but we do not see the growth taking place. So too it should be with spiritual and emotional growth.

One of the necessary conditions for spiritual and emotional growth is human effort. For there to be ongoing development, there must be a significant ongoing input from us. We must go on asking, seeking and knocking. I have yet to know a person who continued to grow spiritually without perseverance in seeking.

Of course there will be disappointments. Of course there will be obstacles. Of course, there will be times when you will find spiritual events boring, when they give you a pain in your head or your back or some other part of your anatomy. Of course, there will be times when you won't feel in the mood to go to Mass or to meetings. Of course there will be times when you feel you are making no progress.

But the appropriate response to experiencing a time of dryness, to feeling that one is making no progress is certainly not to give up. The appropriate response is to broaden and enrich one's efforts; sometimes it is to take one's courage into one's hands and, learning to depend on Jesus, to do things that one has told oneself that one can't do.

There are 10 steps through which we grow spiritually and through which we become open to what Jesus desires to do in our lives. If even one of the ten is missing, our spiritual development will be either retarded or unbalanced or both.

The 10 steps to growth

1. Personal prayer; spending quality time with Jesus each day. Ask the Holy Spirit to show you how much time He desires you to spend in daily prayer, then be loyal to it.

2. Ongoing inner conversion as we seek to allow the light of Jesus to penetrate every area of our mind and heart; starting with repentance of sin and dealing with whatever anger is in one's life.

3. Fellowship with others who have truly come to know Jesus, and who, in harmony with God's plan for His Church, are seeking to become open to everything that God has to offer.

4. Seeking to have the sacraments truly come to life, including joining with Jesus in His offering of Himself to the Father through the Mass and seeking to truly eat His flesh and drink His blood.

5. Putting our prayer into practice through a life of faith, love and generosity, and dependence on God.

6. Spiritual reading - including the New Testament, and also tapes.

7. Sacrifice and self-denial, starting with abstaining from meat on Fridays.

8. Regularly going to places and events where one's relationship with Jesus will be nourished, places of pilgrimage, conferences, retreats, etc.

9. Becoming conscious of one's new family in Christ and learning to treat one's fellow parishioners as real family.

10) Being willing to go the extra mile for God and being willing to take on challenges for the sake of the kingdom.
    If one is married, of course, the first people that one is called to love and to minister to is one's own family.

16

Growth requires fasting

In the early Church, as well as during Lent, they had fast and abstinence every Wednesday and Friday. Their fast meant that they had just one meal which was only eaten in the evening. Their abstinence meant not just abstaining from meat but from all animal products, including milk.

This fasting was taken very seriously. If a person who was connected with the celebration of Mass didn't fast, serious action was taken. If a priest, bishop or deacon didn't fast, he was deprived of his ministry unless there was a serious medical reason. So too with readers and singers. Indeed the person who didn't fast was considered cut off from the sacraments. This is set out in the Didache, a very early Church document.

In the Irish language, the word for Friday literally means the big fast and the word for Wednesday literally means the little fast. So if one is to be in touch with the spirit of the early Church, one needs to fast.

I am not big into fasting, far from it. I do try to abstain from meat on Fridays and normally also either on Wednesdays or, if that isn't possible, on some other day. I also try to keep to a simple moderate diet. Yet, as little fasting as I do, I do experience it as a help. Abstaining from meat on Fridays is a real reminder of the death of Jesus, and it does give one a sense of being united with His offering of Himself to Father for us. It also springs from and leads to an ability to say 'No' to one's own instincts and compulsions.

The abandonment of fasting, and of the concept of sacrifice, has impacted negatively on people's living of their faith in other ways. Food is a major ingredient of living, it is at the heart of life. How we handle our eating and our drinking has a major bearing on the type of person we become. If out of love for God, one learns to say 'Yes' to proper nourishment, but 'No' to self-indulgence in the area of eating and drinking, then there is a great chance that one will continue saying 'Yes' to God and 'No' to self-indulgence in other areas.

Overeating and drinking is symbolic of what is happening throughout the developed world. People have lost the ability to say, 'No', to themselves, and consequently have lost the ability to say, 'Yes', to God, to God's will and to love.

Many have become like a little child that keeps repeating "I want..." Then finding that others are also saying, "I want... I want", they become hardened in their selfishness, and, "I want", changes to, "We demand". They then band together to make their demands like the Israelites demanding the golden calf in the desert. Instead of seeking to discern God's will, they take opinion polls to see the will of the people, and then get lists of signatures for their demands.

It is no coincidence that celibacy has come under attack, and that many priests are finding the living of celibacy either difficult or meaningless, at the same time as the Church has effectively abandoned fasting. Neither is it a coincidence, that the age in which the Church effectively abandoned fasting, is the age of addiction, when so many people are addicted to something or other:- work, pleasure, wealth, sex, drink, food gambling, drugs etc. Neither is it a coincidence that the age in which the Church effectively abandoned fasting is the age of divorce, though it takes time to realise that there is a connection, and there are many other causative factors leading to divorce.

Jesus fasted. On one occasion He even fasted for 40 days. He expected his disciples to fast. "When you fast" He said; not "if you fast". The early Church took fasting very seriously. So did the Church for almost 2,000 years.

The reason fasting became undermined was that people were fasting for the wrong reasons. In a Church that had lost sight of the need for rebirth and inner transformation, lost sight indeed of Jesus being the Bread of Life, it was inevitable that the meaning and purpose of fasting got lost.

Fasting in the first place is about being united with Jesus in His offering of Himself to Father. It is a way of becoming united with Jesus in His death. Uniting oneself with Him in His death, is an important step towards becoming open to Father's love; becoming open indeed to the same power that raised Jesus from the dead, and that can now raise us from our deadness.

Fasting should also be an expression of true conversion, a turning from selfishness and sin. The person who fasts, while he may have blind spots, while he may even be in denial in some key area of life, yet shows that his heart is open, that he desires to deny self in order to become open to God's love.

I have shared how in 1987 I had an unexpected and mysterious experience of coming to see celibacy as a gift rather than as a burden, and of being cleansed sexually, freed from sexual compulsions. I wasn't even thinking or praying about either sex or celibacy prior to this experience, but it happened while I was spending a couple of days in solitude, prayer and moderate fasting.

My opting for a couple of days of prayer, solitude and fasting left me open to the transforming power of God. It is only now that I have suddenly realised that this gentle experience, which has made such a contribution to my living of my priesthood over the past twelve years, occurred on the only occasion in my ministry, when I took a few days to go aside totally on my own for solitude, prayer and fasting.

The Acts of the Apostles recounts how in the early Church, they had an experience of guidance, possibly unexpected guidance, while fasting.

"While they were worshipping the Lord and fasting, the Holy Spirit said, 'Set apart for me Barnabas and Saul for the work to which I have called them.' Then after fasting and praying they laid their hands on them and sent them off" Acts 13:2-3.

Here we see that fasting was normal in the early Church. It wasn't that a special fast was called, but rather that, during one of the normal times for fasting, they received this guidance. Then after receiving the word concerning Barnabas and Saul, there was more fasting to call down God's blessing.

The early Church also fasted when seeking to come under God's anointing. When leaders were being appointed to the local Churches, God's blessing was sought through fasting.

"When they had appointed elders for them in every church, with prayer and fasting, they committed them to the Lord in whom they believed" Acts 14:23.

Fasting helps to leave one open to Father's love, and it makes it possible for Jesus to touch us and to help us with the process of rebirth and inner transformation. Hence one should bring to one's fasting, the desire to be freed from one's compulsions, the desire for deliverance and inner healing. Doing this will be a help towards becoming open to the fruit of the Spirit.

St. Paul rightly says,

"The desires of the flesh are against the Spirit, and the desires of the Spirit are against the flesh" Galatians 5:17.

For many, many years, even after Jesus came into my life, the fruits of the Spirit were just a list in the Bible for me. I read them, I spoke about them, I desired them, I prayed for them, but I didn't really experience them.

Before I could experience the joy which the Holy Spirit desired to bestow upon me, I had to go through a process of inner transformation, healing and growth. Today, I thank God that my life is full of joy and I have a much increased capacity to love.

I've found self-control the most difficult fruit to experience, and without self-control, there cannot be patience. This is a spin-off from all the anger that was in my life. It is only in recent years that I have realised how this damaged my self-control, left me needing ongoing healing in that area. I used to pray for patience, pray to be rid of a hot temper, but what I really needed was inner self-control, the healing of my inner fuse.

It is important, therefore, to inter-link one's fasting from food with one's desire for inner healing and deliverance.

God as love

Around 1960 there developed a greater understanding of God as love. This was perhaps the greatest single development in theology in the twentieth century. But there have been many aberrations based on faulty understandings of love.

One understanding goes something like this,
'God is love, so therefore God wants the very best for us. Therefore He doesn't want anything that would involve any form of suffering. Therefore anything that involves sacrifice or self-denial is wrong, even heretical.'
Others simply dismiss fasting with the declaration, 'Sure you will suffer enough anyway.'

Both statements sound good and even logical, but they overlook two important details.

1) That there is selfishness within the human condition, and that, left unchecked, this selfishness will manifest itself in a host of different ways - including clouding our relationship with God. It is a selfish love that pampers and spoils, and God's love isn't selfish. God's love is a strong love, a challenging love. Jesus offered Himself completely in life and in death to Father for us. We are invited to join in this self-giving offering.

2) Fasting is a very special way of being united with the death of Jesus. In becoming united with Jesus in His death, Father's love which raised Jesus from death can bring a real resurrection in our lives also.

Authentic Christian fasting is motivated by love, and by a desire to grow in love. Just like celibacy. It is easy to have fasting without celibacy, but it isn't easy to have celibacy without fasting. How can the person who has rejected the very notion of sacrifice begin to understand the meaning of celibacy? How helpful it will be for fidelity in celibacy on the other hand, as indeed for fidelity within marriage, if one is already accustomed to saying 'no' to one's desires and impulses in the course of fasting.

If, out of a desire to become open to God, one takes on fasting on a voluntary basis, one develops personal strength, develops an ability to take control and to be in control.

Anorexics discover this value that derives from fasting, but, for them, it becomes an end in itself. Because of confusion in other areas of their lives, they have a compulsive need to experience a sense of control through not eating. They crave this feeling of control. It becomes destructive. Had they grown up in an environment in which Christian fasting was encouraged, their fasting would have had, as its primary goal, uniting with Jesus in His death. It would have been within a structured atmosphere which yet gave them the positive experience of self control. And, ironically, by reverse psychology, those who tend to under eat often develop a very healthy appetite when fasting is mentioned!!!

Fasting out of love for God involves saying "No" to one's desire to pamper self. It fosters a spirituality in which self doesn't come first, a spirituality in which sacrifice is given its true meaning, a spirituality that, incidentally, goes hand in hand with celibacy.

Its knock on effects are many - a greater sense of control over oneself and one's life direction, a greater ability to say "No" to impulses and desires, not to speak of the greater closeness it brings to God and a greater openness to hearing his voice and discerning His will. How hard it is to even pray on an over full tummy!

Very often our physical health will even improve. Many of us are overweight! Sometimes we are being poisoned by all we eat and drink - as I discovered myself when I discovered that health problems I had experienced for years were the result of an allergy I had developed through drinking tea far too often.

Appropriate fasting should be in the context of healthy eating and living habits. The gap should not be filled by that which is itself unhealthy - like several extra cigarettes or mugs of tea or coffee.

Fasting in the first place is to unite us with the death of Jesus. How appropriate then that we begin with something like abstaining from meat on Fridays. One can then consider further steps.

17

The need for stimulus And challenge

One day, some months before my ordination, while I was thinking about what type of ministry I should focus on, I happened to glance down at a book that lay open in front of me. A sentence literally leaped from the page, "Our calling is to devote ourselves to prayer and to preaching." These words lit up, stood out. I knew then, beyond a shadow of a doubt, that God was calling me to a life centred on prayer and preaching.

As a result, I applied to go to the Mission House in Enniscorthy. I thought that that was where I was to live out this calling. God had other ideas! After just three years, I found myself being transferred to the curacy of Murrintown. At the time, it was a major blow. I had felt that preaching parish missions and retreats was my calling and I loved doing it. The move hit very deeply. It was as if my very calling was being taken from me. I was both upset and angry at the time.

Thankfully, while I couldn't see how the transfer could be God's will, I was just about able to see that, whatever God's original will, it was now His will that I accept the change.

When I look back, I can now see things from a very different perspective. The Mission House has been closed down for several years, while I am involved in the ministry of preaching in a different way, through the monthly magazine, the Curate's Diary. Indeed the Curate's Diary is now reaching far more people than I could ever have reached giving parish missions.

Furthermore the sentence that had leaped from the page, "Our calling is to devote ourselves to prayer and to preaching", was from a reflection on Acts 6:4, "We will devote ourselves to prayer and to preaching." Years later I discovered that a more correct translation of that sentence is,

"We will devote ourselves to prayer and to the ministry of the word"
Acts 6:4.

The ministry of the word is certainly at the centre of my life and work today.

Being moved from the Mission House has taught me an important lesson - that God's will isn't necessarily what I believe at the time to be God's will, that God can see the bigger picture. This leaves one humble, more open to embracing change, more willing to listen to suggestions and ideas.

The gap in my life

When I moved from the Mission House to the curacy of Murrintown, there was a big gap in my life. I was moving from living in a community to living on my own in a big house, but above all, I missed the preaching.

At first, I really put my heart into house visitation and into finding ways of being with my parishioners. I had already a deep faith in the living presence of Jesus in my life and also a reasonable prayer life. Both have grown immensely since, but for a young priest, they were then quite good. Yet I didn't find parish work totally fulfilling. In some way that I wasn't able to understand, I needed more, needed something else, something deeper. I knew that something was missing, but I couldn't put my finger on it.

I would, at the time, have identified it as a frustration at the lack of spiritual results; that I wasn't succeeding in helping people grow closer to Jesus. In this, parish work moves at a different level to giving parish missions, as, on Parish Missions, one is continuously challenging people and sharing with them.

But there was another factor also which I was able to see later with the benefit of hindsight:- that some of my mental abilities weren't then being utilised and that, without my knowing it, this was creating a gap, a need. This need couldn't just be filled by any type of work.

Later I became involved in building a Community Centre. In the year or so when I was deeply caught up in this work and fund-raising for it, I was very busy, but I just knew that it wasn't where God was wanting me, that indeed it was keeping me from being where God wanted me to be. Again and again the inner voice kept saying, "This isn't God's plan for you," but I didn't feel that I could listen.

The work on the Community Centre was done under a Government employment scheme. It was for us to supply the materials and to supervise the work. There was a lot of haulage and procuring involved, a lot of running around. Once one starts something like that, one has to keep going. So even though I knew that this wasn't where God wanted me, I felt obliged to see it through.

God has his own ways. If He can't get through to us one way, if we refuse to listen to His voice, then He may just allow something else to happen to get us to where He wants us. If we are outside His will for us, that in itself automatically stops the anointing, stops the flow of blessings, and that in turn has consequences. Differences of opinion arose during the construction of the centre, some due to my own inexperience and mistakes. As a result, I stepped down as chairperson as soon as the building work was completed, and while this was painful at the time, I became available again for the work to which God was calling me.

Over the years I had found existing Catholic magazines and newspapers disappointing. I wrote lengthy letters to a couple of editors with suggestions and criticisms. One Friday evening at the end of March 1985, I had posted a letter to the editor of one such magazine. My letter ran to thirteen pages, mostly critical.

Just after posting it, the thought came to me, almost like an inner voice, "If you are so critical of others, why don't you do something yourself?" That Friday evening I started writing. By Monday evening, the first issue of the Curate's Diary was ready for printing. It was only small, just 12 pages typed on a portable Brother typewriter by my then part-time secretary, Imelda Kirby; 200 copies run off for me by the late Fr. Sean Fortune on his photocopier.

Fr. Sean's ministry ended in tragic circumstances later. I will always remember the fact that it was through his generosity that the first issue of the Curate's Diary was printed. May he rest in peace.

From the moment I started doing the Curate's Diary, I noticed a change in myself. Some inner need was now being met. I believe that it was the need for mental challenge, that there was an important element of my mind that was not being challenged by routine parish work. The thinking required in doing the Diary stimulated my brain and challenged it to its maximum capacity. Better still, it was now being used where I felt God's call - at the service of the kingdom. The sense of something missing, that I had previously experienced, disappeared.

I once heard a mother explaining her reasons for taking up part-time work in similar terms; that she felt that part of her mental ability wasn't being utilised; that she felt a need for an extra dimension to her life. I could understand what she was saying.

It is possible that many people, including many priests, are suffering as I suffered. Many people have to do boring repetitive work that can be soul destroying, while I believe that many priests need a second form of ministry, something that will challenge them in a different way. I believe, indeed, that bishops should have a policy of trying to encourage their priests to broaden their work.

I have come to believe that many younger priests would greatly benefit from having a suitable second portfolio, over and above parish work. The emphasis has to be on 'suitable'; a portfolio that suits their personality, one that will provide them with something of the mental stimulus and spiritual challenge that they need. If it isn't suitable in this sense, it will be a burden rather than a boost.

One has many God-given abilities and capacities. We are at our healthiest when the most advanced of our capacities are being used - though active physical work can be equally satisfying. If either the body or the mind is being stretched to the maximum in the right way, it is good. If both are being stretched, it is better still.

Sometimes this may not be possible. When that happens, it is important to identify and acknowledge the capacity or ability that isn't being used or challenged. Perhaps one may find an alternative outlet for it, or, if not, having acknowledged it, one can, at least, make the conscious decision to offer up the lack for the greater good.

Growing in faith through facing challenges

Then there is the importance of challenge for growing in one's faith. The best way to grow in faith, is to do things that require stepping out in faith. To grow in practical faith, there is a need for ongoing challenges. If one just keeps doing what one has been doing, just as one has been doing it, where is the challenge? That is, unless the task in question, has ongoing challenges built into it.

A great incentive to faith in God is to be continuously seeking to do that which one knows one hasn't, humanly speaking, the ability or the power to do. In the process, one is brought into a deeper relationship with Jesus. Knowing that, without Jesus, what one is doing is impossible, one seeks to depend on Him more and more. That in turn brings one deeper and deeper into prayer. Because one truly knows one's need for Jesus, one also knows that one needs to spend more and more time with Him.

That, in turn, helps one to walk in a right relationship with Him. One gradually learns that, if one isn't walking in a right relationship with Jesus, it has an impact, that one's efforts are not being blessed in the same way.

For many years, I have been aware that an important factor in the circulation of the Curate's Diary, is my own spiritual progress, my own personal holiness or lack of it. After an initial spurt, the circulation dropped from an early peak of 1,200 to about 700 copies and was continuing to decline. Then I had my experience of sexual healing and took other important steps to put my life right before God. Within 12 months, the circulation doubled to 1,500 and it is now close to 8,000 (1999) and is continuing to grow.

Whenever we go through a temporary slump, I always check my own life:- check my loyalty to prayer, my attitudes, whether there is something that needs sorting out or putting right. I also check that what I am writing is in tune with the will of God. It may not be any of these things that is causing the slump, but I always check, because I have learned that they really count.

When I was in Murrintown, the front door faced directly into the prevailing wind and rain. Sometimes the doorbell would corrode internally and so it wouldn't work, as the electricity couldn't flow through it. If it stopped working, I knew where to check for corrosion. In the same way, anytime God's blessings appear to stop flowing in my life, I know where to check for the corrosion.

People think that what they do in private is their own private business. This can never be so for the Christian. Our very calling, as Christians, is to be channels of God's blessing, to incarnate the love of God, and to allow it to flow through us. The flow of God's blessings will be greatly reduced, if not stopped altogether, if one isn't continuously seeking to open one's heart to God, or if one is tolerating any form of sin.

Living in a situation where one continuously depends on God, is a great help to taking growth in personal holiness very seriously. This, in turn, leads to healing and to spiritual maturing.

Turning to Jesus, learning to depend on Him, spending time with Him is a powerful way of opening oneself to His healing love. The healing may be like the growth in the grass, not visible to the human eye, but when one looks back, after walking closely with Jesus for a period, then one can see something of the healing and maturity that has taken place.

18

Victory over one's inhibitions

People sometimes comment about how easy I find it to compose prayers or how easy I find it to preach. Few realise what I had to go through to reach that stage. When I was ordained first, I was both extremely shy and extremely nervous. My personal self-confidence had been broken. So too had my confidence in my ability to speak. My elocution professor had managed to convince me that my elocution was terrible. He hadn't succeeded in showing me how to improve it!

There I was as a young priest, extremely shy, suffering deep feelings of inferiority, finding it difficult to speak in public and knowing that my elocution was a disaster. No wonder I suffered much stress! Stress has a knock-on effect on one's entire personality. It leaves one with a greater need for close friendship and it leaves one more vulnerable to sexual frustration.

During this time I was preaching parish missions. For me, that was a major challenge. Going out to face the people was difficult, frightening. I found that there was only one way I could succeed. I learned that, if I allowed an image of Jesus into my mind and kept it before me, then by relying on Him, I would be able to go out and preach, even preach well.

That was the only way in which I could do it, with an image of Jesus in my mind, depending on Him. Just like the Israelites were led through the desert by the pillar of light, so with an image of Jesus as the pillar of light in the top of my head, I could do things that otherwise were beyond me.

"The Lord went before them by day in a pillar of cloud to lead them
along the way, and by night in a pillar of fire to give them light"
Exodus 13:21.

In every bit as real a way, Jesus went before me every time I stood up to speak, not that He was giving me any special favours. What He did for me, He is more than willing to do for you.

It was a good faith lesson also. It taught me, in a very practical way, how to depend on Jesus and it also taught me a very valuable method of imaging prayer, that is how to use mental images to become open to Jesus and to the blessings that He desires to give. In difficult situations I always fall back on this method.

Today, thankfully, I have great confidence but I still depend on Jesus. I still normally go out to preach with His image in my mind's eye, but I do so with joyful confidence instead of with a nervous fear. Indeed I now hold the image in my mind's eye, not so much for the strength, but out of a desire that what I say be penetrated and anointed by Him. And every so often, I continue to learn what happens when I don't seek to depend on Jesus; how, when I go out in my own strength, I do very badly.

I also found it very hard to mix. My teenage experiences had left me shy and withdrawn and this, in turn, had left me lacking in communication skills and with a tendency to feel inferior.

Once again I had to learn to depend on Jesus, to go into situations with His image in my mind's eye, depending on Him for the power to do that which of myself I couldn't do. For many years it wasn't easy, but it has left me with a great line of communication with the Higher Power. I learned that by depending on Jesus and keeping my inner eye on Him, I could do things, enter situations and meet people when, of myself, I could not do so.

Learning to share

Despite the fact that I had a profound spiritual experience at a Prayer Meeting and a deep ongoing sense of Jesus' love and presence, I also found sharing at Prayer Meetings particularly difficult at first. His love was filling my inner being, yet I found it very difficult to share.

Any time I did share, I was so self-conscious about my own

sharing, and so caught up in wondering about whether my sharing was okay, that it appeared to destroy the whole meeting for me, and so I quickly lapsed back into remaining silent during meetings.

If one doesn't share at meetings, the inevitable will eventually happen. One will end up finding the meetings boring and feel that one is getting nothing out of them. It doesn't matter how deeply the Lord has touched one's life, if one doesn't share, doesn't begin to pass on something of what one has received, the anointing will be lifted and boredom will eventually set in.

It is God's will that every person learns to share. St. Paul teaches, *"At the name of Jesus every knee should bow, in heaven and on earth and under the earth, and every tongue confess that Jesus Christ is Lord, to the glory of God the Father" Philippines 2:9-11.*

"If you confess with your lips that Jesus is Lord, and believe in your heart that God raised Him from the dead, you will be saved" Romans 10:9.

Confessing with one's lips is a necessary step if one is to grow in God's anointing. Some find it very hard, others find it harder still. Yet, if one is capable of speaking, one can, with God's help, become capable of praying aloud. Jesus understands how difficult it is for us, yet it is such a vital step, He won't allow us to just stay as we are. If one is not willing to step out in faith, the anointing will eventually be withdrawn, and natural boredom will set in.

It happened to me within a year of my initial experience. I felt that I was getting nothing out of the meetings, found them boring and heavy going, and so I started to go only occasionally. That was the situation when I was ordained.

After ordination, despite having found them heavy going, I was still interested in Prayer Meetings. After all, it was at one that Jesus touched my life in such a profound way. So I started going to meetings in Co. Wexford.

My contribution to the Prayer Meetings, that I attended in the first few years of my priesthood, was very limited. I was too shy, that is too caught up in myself, and still too broken to be of any real use. There were so many things still to be worked out in my own life that I wasn't open to deep anointing. However, with time,

I began to change. For one thing, a priest is automatically expected to share at Prayer Meetings. My contributions were pretty limited, but gradually I improved.

While the first important step is to learn to share at Prayer Meetings, once one finds sharing easy, the next essential step is to learn to get the Holy Spirit to edit one's sharing. If you find sharing easy and share regularly, always check with the Holy Spirit before sharing - including the sharing of prayer intentions.

Becoming Witnesses

Jesus clearly linked receiving the Holy Spirit to two things. He linked it firstly to loving Him and keeping the commandments.

"If you love me, you will keep my commandments. And I will pray the Father, and He will give you another Counsellor, to be with you for ever" John 14:15-16.

The person with serious sin is just not capable of great openness to the Holy Spirit. Jesus may possibly be in the person's life, so too may the Holy Spirit, but the level of anointing will be greatly determined by how one is facing up to whatever needs facing.

Secondly Jesus linked receiving the Holy Spirit to witnessing.

"When the Counsellor comes, whom I send to you from the Father, ..., He will bear witness to me; and you also are witnesses."

Other Bibles, like the Jerusalem Bible, translate that as "And you too will be witnesses."

Before His ascension, Jesus also declared,

"You shall receive power when the Holy Spirit has come upon you; and you shall be my witnesses" Acts 1:8.

There is a degree to which the Holy Spirit can only be given to those who are willing to be His witnesses. There are, of course, different ways of witnessing, of bringing God's love to people. It is unlikely to involve getting up at a street corner, but it will involve a willingness to share one's faith.

If one refuses to be a witness, one blocks the work of the Holy Spirit in one's own life. The block will not be total, but yet it may be severe. One will be going around with a main spiritual artery blocked - and bypass surgery just isn't possible. The opening of the artery, or should I say the loosening of the tongue is the only way forward.

A light bulb cannot light unless the electricity flows through it. It is the electricity flowing through it that causes it to light. So too with us, if we are to light up, to glow, through the release of the fruits of the Holy Spirit in our lives, it will only be when we are willing to be witnesses in what we do and what we say.

If one declares that one cannot witness, one is really declaring that one is not willing to be a witness; that one is not prepared to go through the pain or suffer the embarrassment. I am not suggesting that learning to speak of one's faith is easy. I certainly did not find it easy. I am saying, rather, that it is necessary.

We need in the first place to learn to talk to Jesus and to talk to Father. What sort of relationship does one have with Jesus and Father, if one isn't prepared to talk to them in one's own words?

Imagine if one decided that one would only communicate with one's earthly father, by using words that others had written. One would be considered totally odd, dysfunctional! So too in our relationship with God. Jesus desires to be our very best Friend, and He desires that we know Father as Abba, Daddy. But for those relationships to develop, we need to be able to talk to Jesus as a real person and so too with Father.

Secondly we need to learn to talk to God in the presence of others. Don't even expect to be brilliant at it at first. It is far better to make up one's mind that one is going to be content with a few words badly spoken. Of course, it will be difficult. Of course, one will find it painful. But, if one shares even a few broken words with a sincere heart, the Holy Spirit can take them and bring real blessing out of them.

Most Prayer Groups made one major mistake in the early days - they appointed the most eloquent people to be leaders. People were appointed leaders either because of who they were, or because of how they could speak, rather than because of how their lives were touched. Is it any wonder that so many groups made such little progress! It was trusting in position and eloquence rather than in the Holy Spirit.

Prayer Meetings should not be about eloquence. Of course, if a person who has truly been touched by the spirit, either is eloquent or has become eloquent, that is nice. But even that person's eloquence can lead to the temptation to start judging prayers in terms of their eloquence.

The central purpose of Prayer Meetings is to become open to and to grow in the transforming power of Jesus, the outpouring of the Holy Spirit, and the love of Father. Eloquence can help or it can hinder. But every person is of equal importance, and the few words humbly spoken by the person who finds it difficult to speak, is as likely to produce an anointing of God's power, as the eloquent words of a fluent speaker.

So, if you find it difficult to speak, go to Jesus for help. Repent of and renounce all the declarations that you have made claiming that you are incapable of speaking. God has given you a tongue. Now consecrate it to Him, that it may be used to bring Him praise.

Thirdly learn to talk to your friends about Jesus and about spiritual things. Again it will not be easy. Start with one's best friends, then progress.

Fourthly, learn to freely praise God aloud - including in the company of others. Here in Ireland our ancestors had to worship in total silence for several hundred years. It was very dangerous for them to make noise during Mass. This has imprinted itself on the way the Mass is celebrated in Ireland down to the present day. That is understandable. But now we must break through the cycle of inhibitions.

Going into Church doesn't make one a participant in Mass no more than going to a football pitch makes one a footballer.

Every person is called by God to participate, to get involved, to answer up, to join in the singing. If one desires to become open to the Holy Spirit, this is a basic step. The chief reason people don't sing in Church, is that, spiritually, they have nothing to sing about. If one's spirit is truly being filled with joy by the Holy Spirit, singing will be inevitable.

19

Facing sexual temptation

During my time in seminary, I did quite an amount of agonising over celibacy. I had discussed sexuality and my capacity to live a celibate life with my spiritual director. But in my thinking about sexuality and celibacy, it had never even entered my head that I would find myself seeking to be loyal to celibacy in situations in which I was being solicited sexually.

This was as far from my thoughts as was the existence of paedophile priests! One just didn't think that such things happened and so there was no plan for how to deal with them.

It is one thing deciding for celibacy in the quiet of one's seminary room without a woman within half a mile. It is another thing living that decision for celibacy when one is faced with a woman, perhaps even a highly attractive woman, begging one to have a sexual relationship.

Often saying 'No' at the time of being solicited is the easiest part. Living that 'No' in the weeks after being solicited is the hardest. I remember one occasion in particular. I had given a mission well over 100 miles from Co. Wexford. During it, I had briefly spoken to a young woman on one occasion, in the Church, after the ceremony was over. It was a brief conversation with people around us.

After I returned to Enniscorthy, she made an appointment to come see me. I must admit that I was flattered, felt that I was really making it as a preacher. After all, it wasn't every day that someone travelled over 100 miles for advice or counselling!

I won't go into all the gruesome details. But 20 minutes into her visit, I discovered it most certainly was not for spiritual advice that she had come! Indeed I discovered it in a very big way! Nor was she quick to accept 'No' for an answer - indeed quite the contrary. She was very attractive physically and had appeared totally normal up to that point. She had an outgoing bubbly personality. I was only two years ordained. I was still finding sexuality a major struggle. I have to admit that I was tempted, but I did manage to say 'No'.

Saying 'No' while she was there was one thing, continuing to live that 'No' in the weeks and months afterwards was much more difficult. There was ongoing temptation, even pain and frustration. Luckily, the following day, I left for a two week mission in a county very far from the one in which she lived.

I was then still quite inexperienced in relationships with the opposite sex, which meant I was also inexperienced in recognising warning signs. It never entered my head that ladies would be sexually interested in priests, that some would even solicit priests. Indeed it took quite a while for the realisation to truly sink home.

The truth is that all Christian leaders, married and single, can expect to be solicited several times. Sometimes it will come totally out of the blue. One may have given a talk or talks somewhere or perhaps gone on a pilgrimage. Later one gets a phonecall. The person wants an appointment.

On the surface it seems totally innocent. At first the visit may appear totally normal, though, with experience, one may detect warning signs in the way the person is dressed and in elements of subtle flirtation. But eventually one discovers the truth, that it isn't one's counselling skills or spiritual insights that has caused the person to come, but, rather, because they are physically attracted.

Some go straight to the point. The incident I shared is one of three occasions on which I found myself being solicited by a person that I didn't even know personally. Others move a much slower pace, but one eventually discovers that the underlying reason for the visits isn't counselling or spiritual advice. The real reason for the person coming back again and again is sexual attraction.

Sometimes one may be lucky in that the person finds it easier to solicit over the phone. One starts to get very explicit phone calls from them - sometimes in the middle of the night. Again it may be from a person with whom one has had only the most fleeting contact.

Where there is sexual attraction, even if the sexual attraction is on one side only, conversation tends to become very easy. One finds the person charming, a lovely person with whom to talk. This is because the person who is experiencing the physical attraction is on a high, their brain is stimulated, there is great alertness.

When one isn't conscious of the real dynamics that are taking place, when one isn't able to recognise physical attraction for what it really is, one is unprepared and as a result, more vulnerable.

Of course, recognising the dynamics of what is taking place is only a help if one is prepared to look at the situation in the cold light of day and, in one's mind, clearly renounce the possibility of the relationship becoming more sexual.

Then one needs to follow up with firm steps including creating a bit of distance. There are millions of people in the world, thousands of priests and lay leaders. If there has been any sign of inappropriate suggestions, it is wise to tell the person to go to someone else.

At a subconscious level, a game may even be going on. One or both parties may be testing to see how far he or she can go, to see how open the other is to a further development in the relationship. While the person would be deeply offended if it was suggested that he or she had designs on the other person, yet there are mental fantasies in which a sexual relationship is pictured. These need to be firmly renounced and dealt with.

Other times the solicitation may come from someone that one has known over the years. Perhaps there has been a degree of attraction, but always at the level of normal acquaintance or friendship. Then the person has some form of breakdown or is going through a crisis, or has too much to drink. Late at night, one gets a phonecall begging one to go see them, or else, the person turns up on one's doorstep, again most likely late at night.

Since one knows the person well, it is hard to refuse to see her - especially as there will probably be tears, and sometimes even talk of suicide. Yet from the start, it will inevitably be a difficult situation. Dealing with a deeply distressed member of the opposite sex is always difficult when one is on one's own. One desires to comfort, to express compassion. It is natural that there be some degree of contact.

Then the person may ask to be held. Remember this is someone that one may have known for 10, 20, 30 or 40 years. One's heart is going out to her in her distress. One desires to comfort, to do anything that is appropriate that will bring soothing. All they appear to be asking for is a hug.

But one needs to be firm. Very often, the more one gives, the more is asked. A hug may be okay and maybe that is all they are really seeking, but one needs to be ready for what is likely to come next. A more intimate holding will likely soon be suggested. There will likely also be the suggestion that far more than just a hug is available.

All Christian leaders can expect to face this. But the priest is at an extra disadvantage in that he is expected to work alone. It isn't so easy for him to bring another person along. Such a move will be seen as an infringement on the confidentiality. On a couple of occasions, I secretly phoned for a priest friend to come, when a woman turned up at my house late at night. The arrival of a second priest was never taken well by the female visitor! Quite the opposite in fact.

In recent years, my workload is such, that I have had to greatly reduce both my speaking engagements and my counselling engagements, but in so far as I do still agree to counsel, I try to schedule all appointments with eligible females for a time that my secretary is also in the house.

Satan's role

Apart from one's hormones and natural sexual attraction, there is also a further factor - satan knows exactly where one is weak. If one is struggling sexually, satan knows about it. He knows where one is weak, where one has a blind spot, where one is open to compromise, where one has inner compulsions.

Where a person has yielded to a serious habit of sin and is indulging in it, satan can prompt that person as to where and when to act. Without their even realising it, satan will lead them to where they can do the most hurt.

Did you ever notice how break-ins at one's home are more likely to take place while one is in a Church or at a Prayer Meeting, than when one is in a pub? Or how thieves often appear very lucky, striking at the right moment? I believe that this is because the thief, having surrendered that area of his or her life to satan's influence, has the benefit of his prompting and guidance. Satan hopes that if he can organise a break-in at one's house while one is in Church, one will be slow to go to Church again. He also delights in having elderly people living in fear, so they too are extra vulnerable.

The same principle applies to the person who is indulging a habit of sexual sin, especially if there is no desire to repent. He or she is also open to satan's inspiration. Satan can and indeed will use him or her for his own purposes. This applies to those priests who have the type of sexual problems that cause them to target others - satan will be there to prompt them where to find their victim and where to do the most hurt.

It equally applies to the woman who is controlled by her sexual compulsions. Satan can use her to bring hurt, whether it be to target a married man, or a Christian leader or a priest; and satan knows exactly who is most open to being tempted.

Thus if a priest or a Christian leader is struggling sexually, he or she can expect to be sexually tempted; can expect that satan will raise up people to solicit sex or a sexual relationship.

Satan also works in another way. We are very familiar with satan's role as tempter, but what we are often unaware of is that he is also the accuser. The Bible describes him as the "accuser of our brethren".

"The accuser of our brethren has been thrown down, the one who accuses them day and night before our God" Rev. 12:10.

Satan loves to accuse because he is out to destroy. It is his very nature. If he cannot destroy us by tempting us, he will then try to do so by accusing us. Any Christian leader who becomes in any way involved in a wrong relationship, can expect that it will come back to haunt him or her. Satan will see to that.

Christian leaders, indeed all Christians, need also to be very clear that a wrong relationship, or any form of inappropriate activity, blocks the work of the Holy Spirit, and hence blocks God's anointing and the outpouring of God's blessings both upon oneself and upon one's ministry.

"The desires of the flesh are against the Spirit, and the desires of the Spirit are against the flesh" Galatians 5:17.

The first three "works of the flesh" listed by St. Paul are immorality, impurity and licentiousness, (Galatians 5:19). St. Paul continues,

"I warn you, as I warned you before, that those who do such things shall not inherit the kingdom of God" Galatians 5:21.

Inheriting the kingdom of God refers in the first place to becoming open to God's anointing, God's blessings. These blessings include the fruit of the Spirit. One will neither see God's anointing upon one's ministry, nor will one experience the fruit of the Spirit, if one tolerates serious sexual sin.

A wrong relationship always involves serious sexual sin! Indeed not merely will one not experience any depth of the fruits of the Spirit while such sin persists, but, even after one repents, much healing needs to take place before the fruits truly flow.

Father's plan is for us to experience real healing in our sexuality. He desires total freedom for us from sexual compulsions and total freedom from sexual fantasies. Not merely does He desire it, but He makes it possible for those who are prepared to go on seeking it.

20

Living alone

One image that has really affected people's view of priestly celibacy, is the image of the 'poor priest' living 'all alone' in the 'big empty house'. Many priests do live alone in a big house, and it isn't a nice experience to come back, tired and worn out, to a house that may have many signs of not being lived in; no light on, no fire lighting, perhaps a considerable degree of untidiness.

This image is often evocatively captured in T.V. programmes as different priests share their personal lived experiences. People were so deeply moved by one recent T.V. presentation that they cried. But there is nothing in the Bible which says that a priest must live either alone or in a big empty house. Neither is there anything in Church teaching which says that a priest must live either alone or in a big empty house. Neither is there anything in tradition which indicates that a priest must live either alone or in a big empty house. Quite the contrary.

The priest living 'alone' in a big 'empty' house is a very modern phenomena. Even in living memory, not merely did a rural priest normally have a live-in housekeeper, but, very often also, he had a live-in male worker who looked after the priest's horse and livestock. This three person set-up was the norm in many parts up to fifty years ago.

In Genesis we read, "Then God said, 'It is not good that the man should be alone" (Gen. 2:18). The recognition of man's need for companionship is thus placed at the very beginning of the Bible. It is a basic human need.

Jesus was celibate. But He did not live on His own or in isolation. During His ministry He travelled with the group. *"The twelve were with Him, and also some women who had been*

healed of evil spirits and infirmities: Mary, called Magdalene, from
whom seven demons had gone out, and Joanna, the wife of Chuza,
Herod's steward, and Susanna, and many others, who provided for
them out of their means." Luke 8: 1b-3.

Those who were with Him were His new family.
"Looking around on those who sat about him, He said, "Here are my
mother and my brethren. Whoever does the will of God is my brother,
and sister, and mother!" Mark 3:34.

Note the type of relationship that Jesus omits in this passage.
They are His mother, His brethren, His brother, His sister, but they
are not His wife. The entire Church is His spouse, but not any one
person within it.

The very relationships mentioned, mother, brother, sister,
brethren are all platonic. To have sexual relationships within this
circle is incest. Jesus had companionship, but it was the
companionship of those who share bread, not of those who share
bed. The word 'companion' comes from the Latin words, 'com'
which means 'with' and 'panis' which means 'bread'. A companion
is literally one with whom one shares bread.

Jesus' appreciation of the human need for companionship is to
be seen in His final act on the cross.
"When Jesus saw his mother, and the disciple whom he loved standing
near, he said to his mother, "Woman, behold, your son!" Then he said
to the disciple, "Behold, your mother!" And from that hour the
disciple took her to his own home." John 19: 26-27.

One the one hand the 'beloved disciple', representing all beloved
disciples, receives Mary as mother. But at the very practical level,
the lives of both John, the beloved disciple, and Mary are enriched.
Mary no longer has to fear living alone. Her husband dead, her
only son crucified, she receives a home, family, companionship.

We see here Jesus' care for his beloved mother. This same Jesus
cares for his beloved priests. He does not desire to see them living
alone in big empty houses. On the contrary, Jesus desires that
practical steps be taken to tackle this problem.
"There is no man who has left house or wife or brothers or parents or
children, for the sake of the kingdom of God who will not receive
manifold more in this time" Luke 18: 29-30.

This promise refers to the here and now, but for it to be fulfilled, practical steps need to be taken - just like Jesus took practical steps for His mother.

I have come to believe in celibacy.   But I do not accept or believe that a priest living alone is God's plan for us priests. Neither do I believe that it either springs from, or leads to, the most wholesome living of celibacy.

I am one of the lucky priests. I do the monthly magazine, the Curate's Diary. I combine that with my parish work. As the Curate's Diary grew, it became absolutely necessary for me to have a full time employee.   She is also paid for out of the Curate's Diary account. I can see the difference that having a full-time employee has made to my quality of life. Indeed, I look back to the day I took on my first live-in secretary/homemaker, as a real turning point in my lived experience of the priesthood. My house is now a real home.

I am particularly blessed in the person I now have. When Joanne came first, I treated her as I would a daughter. She has also proved a wonderful friend, yet she has developed her own completely independent life. Having such an employee is a great blessing.

Finding a suitable employee isn't easy.   But even though such people are scarce, because it is God's will to bless us in this way, with prayer, a suitable person will be found. I remember the time I took on Joanne. I had been praying hard to find a suitable person and I felt that certain qualities were needed. As I prayed, an image came into my mind.

The image started with a local person I already knew, a person who had the type of personality I was looking for, but then the image changed to look somewhat like the local person but yet be quite different. It was only a very vague image - I never get clear ones, indeed I very seldom get any image at all. However, when Joanne came for interview, I knew that she was the person represented in the image.

I am aware that the time will come for Joanne to go on to greater things. I live with that realisation but I can only trust that God will provide when that day comes.

Choosing the right person as one's employee is vitally important. Sometimes, out of the goodness of one's heart and out of a genuine desire to help, one ends up offering the position to someone who has problems. That can be disastrous! For everyone! Where a person has been coming to the priest with problems, her need for love and her desire to depend, could create a dynamism that would lead their relationship into the wrong track emotionally, spiritually and possibly physically.

There are two fundamental qualities one should seek in any prospective employee.

A) A capacity for an independent spirit, not seeking to depend or to possess. I am speaking here of emotional dependence rather than a person's need for company. I believe in treating anyone who works in my house as family. But the emotionally dependent person will crave attention, will desire an ever deeper relationship, will gradually become more and more possessive.

B) She should respect and be capable of respecting his celibacy.

Inevitably where one has a live-in employee, much time will be spent together, including times when the priest is tired, drained, vulnerable. For this reason, these basic qualities are absolutely necessary.

The usual reason given for not having a full time employee is that one can't afford one. Yet the solution that is suggested to our living alone is marriage! But if one cannot afford an employee, how on earth will one be able to afford to send one's children to university?

I'm not saying that every priest is, at this time, in a position to pay a full time employee. Where he is not, the situation needs to be remedied. But what is really needed is a whole new attitude involving bishops, priests and laity. It needs to be recognised by all, that the present situation is not God's plan, and the appropriate adjustments need to be made.

Meanwhile an individual priest can only try to create the situation whereby he can take on an employee.

21

Becoming open to Father's love

One time I went to Confession as a teenager with the usual teenage problems. I went to a young priest. He didn't have a reputation for harshness. However he reckoned that I was well on the road to hell. The only hope that he saw for me sprang from the fact that I went to Confession regularly.

Back then, which is just thirty five years ago, we still were dominated by the concept of a vengeful God, a God who punishes. This was a contributory factor to some of the terrible harshness in our religious institutions, some of the physical abuse that took place. As long as people believed in a vengeful God, they too felt free to be vengeful, for, in being vengeful, they were only being like God as they understood Him.

We truly need to exorcise from our minds and hearts every notion of a vengeful God! Jesus revealed that God is love and challenges us to a life centred on love.

"As the Father has loved me, so have I loved you; abide in my love. If you keep my commandments, you will abide in my love." John 15:9-10

"Love your enemies and pray for those who persecute you, so that you may be sons of your Father who is in heaven; for He makes His sun rise on the evil and on the good, and sends rain on the just and on the unjust" Mt. 5:44-45.

If we are to be like God, we must be transfigured by love and become vehicles of love. Yet we must not make the even more fatal mistake of thinking that, since God loves us, it doesn't matter how we behave. God loves us with an infinite love, but that is of no value to us unless we open our hearts to His love and seek to be

transformed by it.   What we do, how we live, is supremely
important.   The prodigal son only became open to his father's
love when he came to his senses and returned to him.
"If anyone loves the world, love for the Father is not in him" 1 John 2:15

We tend to put our entire focus on Jesus, and to forget Father
and the Holy Spirit. But suppose you visited a family of three
persons, and insisted on talking only to one and ignored the other
two, wouldn't it be very odd?   Then suppose your friend started
offering to introduce you to the other two, started asking you to
treat them also as family, and you still showed no interest, wouldn't
it be very bad form. Your friend's home could never truly be your
home until your attitude changed.

Jesus really wants us to meet and know His Family, the Trinity.
He even invites us to call His Father, 'Abba', which literally means
'Daddy', the name a child uses for its father.

Jesus desires that we come to know Father's love, desires that
Father become a very real loving Father for us. But we shy away.
We are prepared to call Father by the Aramaic word 'Abba', but
which of us has the confidence to call Him, 'Daddy' or even 'Dad'.

When Jesus was trying to make a point and saw that it was going
right over the people's heads, He often said something that, for
them, would sound shocking. Trying to shock them into realising
how very real Father should be in their lives, He declared,
*"Call no man your father on earth, for you have one Father who is in
heaven" Matthew 23:9.*

St. Paul's Prayer

Coming to know Father, and becoming open to His power to bless
and transform us, is an important step in spiritual growth. Seeking
to open their hearts to Father, St. Paul offered a very special prayer
for the Ephesians,
*"That the Father of glory, may give you a spirit of wisdom and of
revelation in the knowledge of Him, having the eyes of your hearts
enlightened, that you may know what is the hope to which He has called*

you, what are the riches of his glorious inheritance in the saints, and what is the immeasurable greatness of His power in us who believe, according to the working of his great might which he accomplished in Christ when He raised Him from the dead." Ephesians 1:17-20

He prays first that they would receive a spirit of "wisdom and revelation" to know Father. How we too need to make that prayer both for ourselves and for our Church, that we too may experience a real breakthrough with Father .

St. Paul then prays that you may have "the eyes of your hearts enlightened". Did you know that you have an inner eye? It is this 'eye' which causes words to appear to light up when they have special meaning. We need to have this eye enlightened, so that when we read about Father, and the blessings He has for us, something within us will light up.

Father has far more blessings for us than we are experiencing. St. Paul spells out what the more is in three parts.

1

"That you may know what is the hope to which He has called you."

In other words, that we may know Father's plan for us, His desire to help us to become open to His infinite love that can transform us.

2

"That you may know ... what are the riches of his glorious inheritance in the saints."

Here 'saints', as always in the New Testament, refers to the living not the dead, those who are living their faith here and now. The prayer then is, that we may know how His love has transformed their lives and so can transform our lives also.

This is the glorious inheritance. Imagine inheriting £10,000,000 and never being told about it. That is nothing to inheriting Father's love, with its tremendous power to transform us, and not being told, or, even worse still, being told but failing to collect.

3

"That we may know ... what is the immeasurable greatness of His power in us who believe, according to the working of his great might

which he accomplished in Christ when He raised Him from the dead."

The Greek word here for 'power' is 'dunamis', the word from which we also get the words 'dynamite' and 'dynamic'. So Father's power in us, when we become open to it, is dynamic power, spiritual dynamite. It is indeed the same power with which Father raised Jesus from the dead.

St. Paul is praying that the eyes of our hearts may be enlightened, so that we may know that this dynamic love of Father's, the love which raised Jesus from the dead, can enter our lives also, can bring new life where there is deadness within us, can deliver us from our compulsions, and can truly transform us.

Father has great blessings for those who come to the banquet, those who are willing to go on asking, seeking, and knocking.

Father and the Mass

When I was ordained first, I thought that every time I begun a prayer in the Mass with the title, 'Lord,' that it was to Jesus I was talking. Then one day while offering Mass, it suddenly struck me that many of the Mass prayers started with 'Lord' and finishing with "through Jesus Christ, your son". It was a moment of insight. I suddenly realised that the key prayers of the Mass were addressed to Father, that indeed the Mass itself is offered to Father.

This is a most important realisation. The Mass makes present Jesus' offering of Himself to Father. We join with Jesus in His offering of Himself and unite ourselves to His offering. If one doesn't realise this, one is missing a most important element of the Mass.

In the early Church, people were accustomed to both Father and Jesus being called Lord. Lord was an Old Testament title for God. When the apostles called Jesus 'Lord' they were declaring that He too was God, but they also continued to call Father, 'Lord'. They distinguished between the two by calling Father, 'Lord' and calling Jesus, 'Lord Jesus'. So in the Mass, if the prayer begins with just "Lord", it is most likely to Father that one is praying, whereas if it is addressed to Jesus, it will likely begin with "Lord Jesus".

The Ultimate Intercessory Sacrifice

Jesus gave His life totally and completely for us as the supreme act of love to Father. His entire ministry was directed towards this most radical form of intercession; the giving of his own life in the ultimate intercessory sacrifice, Calvary.

Our vision of Calvary is so dominated by the physical sufferings of Jesus that we fail to see that Calvary is the ultimate act of love; that Jesus is offering Himself completely and totally to Father for us.

"Father, into thy hands I commit my spirit" (Luke 23:46).

It is the moment of total self-giving, offering his very self as a sacrifice in intercession for us. He gives His life in an act of total love to Father. Such was the power involved, that it even caused an earthquake at the moment of his death.

Father receives that self-giving by raising Jesus from the dead. The same power by which Father raised Jesus from the dead is present to us to rise us up, to give us the new life, to set us free from our bondages. How truly so many of us need to be touched by this power and need also a real breakthrough in our relationship with Father.

"And you He (Father) made alive when you were dead through the trespasses and sins" Ephesians 2:1.

In one sense Jesus' self-offering is a once and for all sacrifice, total and complete.

"He offered one sacrifice, once and for all, when he offered himself"
Hebrews 7:27 (GN).

Yet in another sense it is incomplete, for Jesus depends on His followers, on us, to make it present in our own time and place. We are called to incarnate it, to live it out in our own lives. Jesus has placed his mission at our mercy. He now has no hands and no body except ours in this time and space.

Our spiritual life should centre on living out His self-offering to Father, on growing in Father's love. To become in our homes and streets and in our places of work, leisure and entertainment, the incarnation not just of Jesus but of Jesus' self-giving to Father, and then of the power of Father to transform us, resurrect us.

Our spirits can become the junction where Father's love embraces the love of the Son:- Jesus living within us, Father's love surging in. Even realising what we are called to can ignite us, can become like a flash of lightning erupting. Each time we celebrate Mass, we are invited to be at the epicentre of the very force which caused the earth to quake when Jesus died.

The Priest as Intercessor

The Mass is our liturgical participation in the self-giving of Jesus to Father. It is our opportunity to join with Jesus as we offer our very selves to Father. This self-giving isn't just personal, for oneself; it is representative, on behalf of, in intercession for. We are uniting with Jesus as he gives himself in intercession for mankind; uniting with Him in offering ourselves to the Father, uniting also with Him as we raise up the needs of our people, including their need for redemption.

The priest's very vocation demands that he immerses himself in the self-giving of Jesus for mankind, that he too be an intercessor, uniting with Jesus in His ultimate act of intercession Father, interceding for His people that they too may be lifted up to experience Father's love.

Footnote - Celibacy and Intercession

The early Church fathers were deeply aware of the intercessory role of the priest. They also saw a clear link between the priest's intercessory role and his being either celibate or else abstaining from relationships with his wife. Early Church writings abound with the connection. Quotation after quotation leaps from the writings of the early Church Fathers, hammering home the message that the priest is called to a life of intercession and that because of this intercessory role, he is called to a life of special chastity:- St. Jerome, St. Ambrose, Ambrosiaster, Pope Gregory the Great, the Council of Carthage of 419, the Council of Tours of 461, and a host of others emphasise this point.

See Cochini's excellent book, 'The Apostolic Origins of Priestly Celibacy.'

22

Methods for understanding vital Biblical texts

When faced with any controversial Scripture text, it is of vital importance to ask, "How was this text understood in the early Church?" They had the Apostles and the Evangelists to explain the meaning of the texts, to ensure that the people understood them in the correct way. The written word was only part of the teaching mission of the apostles and the evangelists. Sometimes the New Testament writers presumed that the readers already knew certain things. Very often what they wrote was supplemented by what they said and how they lived.

It is therefore impossible to come to a full understanding of vital New Testament texts, without seeking to find out how they were understood and lived, in the early Church.

In 1 Thessalonians we find that the Gospel isn't just the written word but that it includes how it is experienced and lived by the people.

"For our Gospel came to you not only in word, but also in power and in the Holy Spirit and with full conviction" 1 Thess. 1:5.

So the New Testament becomes Gospel, Good News, only when it comes with power and with the Holy Spirit to transform people's lives. What happens in people's lives is a vital element of the Good News, the Gospel. Taking the written word separately to how it was lived and understood is an error.

We see this again in 1 Thess. 2:13.

"When you received the word of God which you heard from us, you accepted it... as the word of God which is at work in you believers."

Besides what the apostles wrote, there was also what they preached orally. The Bible itself teaches,

"So then, brethren, stand firm and hold to the traditions which you were taught by us either by word of mouth or by letter" 2 Thess. 2:15.

This passage is of major importance. Here the Bible itself teaches that one is to be guided by what the apostles taught by word of mouth as well as in writing. If we accept it, then we must accept that those who preach, "Scripture Only", are preaching an un-scriptural doctrine, whereas those who preach Scripture and tradition are preaching what the Bible itself preached.

Finding the value behind the rule

The cornerstone of authentic tradition is how the Bible was understood in the early Church. It doesn't mean that the early Church's understanding of every last detail is binding.

The early Church believed, for example, that women should wear headgear in Church. But yet we don't feel it necessary to uphold this rule. What it is necessary to keep, however, is the value that lay behind the rule:- that we behave in Church in a way that expresses respect and which creates an atmosphere in which others are not distracted.

We retain the value but we don't feel obliged to retain the same rule to uphold it. This is an important principle. It applies to celibacy also. They didn't have compulsory celibacy in the early Church, but instead they expected married priests to be 'continent', that is, to live as brother and sister with their wives.

The rule of marital continence is a different rule to celibacy, but the same two values lie behind both. Both are expressions of the priest being asked to be deeply united with the celibate Jesus, the bridegroom, to be effectively His best man, and both respond to the radical call of Jesus to be willing to leave all to follow Him.

In themselves the rule of celibacy and the rule of continence are Church rules. As Church rules they can be changed. But there are two things which cannot be changed:- the radical call of Jesus for full-time ministers who will leave all to follow Him and the priest's calling to serve as best man for Jesus, the Bridegroom, who gives Himself totally and exclusively for His people.

Like John the Baptist, the priest is "the Bridegroom's friend who .. is glad when he hears the Bridegroom's voice." John 3:29 (GN).

23

The First 350 Years

Around 217 Pope Callistus was bitterly opposed by St. Hippolytus on the basis that, if a member of the clergy got married, Callistus wouldn't have him dismissed. So even around the year 200, there was a rule that priests could not marry, though sometimes this rule was breached.

The Church spread over a wide area in its first 350 years. Indeed it even spread to Ireland! One could divide the early Church into 5 main regions:- Western Europe, Central Europe including Rome, North Africa, Jerusalem, and the East. If we find that something was being taught in every region around the year 350, one could accept with real confidence that this is an authentic Apostolic tradition. How otherwise could it have spread to each region if it didn't come from the common source, the Apostolic Church?

Western Europe

The Council of Elvira was held in Spain sometime between 300 and 309 A.D. Canon 33 concerns clerics "who must live in abstinence with their wives". It lays down that clerics are forbidden to have relations with their wives or procreate children. Anyone who broke this rule was to be suspended.

The very heading shows that this rule was taken for granted. It is concerning clerics "who must live in abstinence with their wives." That is the way things were. The purpose of the canon was to set out both what the rule involved and the penalty for those who broke it.

This is not the type of practice that was likely to spring up from nowhere; certainly not something that was likely to emerge during a period when the Church was enduring persecution. Nor was it the type of regulation that one region would be likely to embark on its own. So we must ask:- Could this rule go right back to the Apostolic times? To the teaching of Jesus Himself? Let us look at Africa.

The Early African Experience

Starting in the year 220, the bishops of North Africa held regular Councils at Carthage. The bishops at the Council of 390 were very clear that "the rule of continence and chastity was discussed in a previous council". They declared that "the rule of continence and chastity" was "what the apostles taught and what antiquity itself observed". They agreed unanimously that all clerics were to abstain from their wives and observe "perfect chastity."
A further Council was held in 419. The 240 African bishops present included St. Augustine. Present also was a papal legate, Faustinus, and two priests from Rome. Bishop Aurelius of Carthage opened the Council with the declaration that they had the documents of the Council of Nicaea before them. This is important, as an effort was later made to claim that Nicaea allowed priests to live the married life. It didn't.

The papal legate, Faustinus, said that all clerics, "those who touch the sacred mysteries, guardians of chastity, abstain with their wives." The bishops unanimously agreed. The Council then declared that all clerics were to "abstain from their wives 'as if they did not have one'". Any cleric who failed to do so was to be dismissed. The bishops were satisfied that what they were teaching was in full conformity with Nicaea.

Here one sees that Rome, Africa and Nicaea had the same understanding of clerical continence. Married men could become priests, but once they did so, they were expected to live a brother - sister relationship with their wives.

Rome And The Popes

Even by the year 150, Rome was being recognised as the centre of orthodoxy within the Church. So it was natural that when questions arose concerning celibacy, they were addressed to Rome. Pope Siricius (384-399) ruled that priests and deacons are bound "by the everlasting law of continence". Severe penalties were set for those who breached this rule. He declared that those clerics, who after ordination still had children, were acting against an irrevocable law which went back to the beginning.

Some pointed to the Old Testament practice, whereby priests only abstained with their wives while actually serving in the temple, and they suggested that priests could have a full marital relationship when not saying Mass. Pope Siricius strongly rejected this. From the day of one's ordination, one was obliged to live in perpetual continence, he declared.

In 386 Pope Siricius wrote to the African bishops outlining what had taken place at a recent synod in Rome. The Synod quoted 2 Thessalonians 2:15,

"Stand firm, and keep the traditions that we taught you whether by word of mouth or by letter."

We see here that it was the understanding in the early Church that it wasn't just the written Scriptures that were to be obeyed, but also what the Apostles said. The Synod, with some 80 bishops present, reaffirmed that priests were forbidden to have sexual relationships with their spouses.

They discussed St. Paul's phrase about the priest being "the husband of one wife". This referred to the priest's position before ordination, they said. After ordination he was expected to live as brother and sister with his wife.

Nor is the Roman evidence confined to the Popes. Both St. Ambrose (339-397), and St. Jerome were equally clear, that while a married man could be ordained, and while he had an obligation to bring up his family properly, he yet was expected to live as brother and sister with his wife. This, Jerome said, was the true meaning of St. Paul's instruction that the priest should be "the husband of only one wife'. He declared that this was the practice in the Eastern Church, the Egyptian Church and the Western Church.

Often in the early Church there was a shortage of priests. In that situation, a married man might find himself pressured to become a priest so that people would not be without Mass. St. Augustine declared that, even in such cases, the married man, who agreed to become ordained under pressure, was yet expected to live as brother and sister with his wife. In this he would be an example to the lay person whose spouse had deserted him, he said.

But does all this mean that the tradition of married priests having to live as brother and sister with their wives went back to the Apostles? The evidence is circumstantial, but it is quite compelling. If it didn't go back to the Apostles, when did it start? How could it have been introduced later without causing a major controversy? Had such a controversy taken place we would definitely have some records of it, just as there are records of all the other major controversies in the early church. And how could it have become so universally accepted? But, you may ask, what about the East?

The Eastern Church

The Council of Nicaea held in 325 is crucial. Those who claim that the custom of married men living in a full marital relationship with their wives was an early Church tradition, claim that it was approved by the Council of Nicaea. However this claim does not stand up to any form of reasonable historical research. It was first made by a lawyer named Socrates who himself wasn't even born until 55 years after the Council. He first made the claim about 100 years after the Council, at a time when abuses were beginning to be tolerated. The Eastern Church over the following 300 years didn't put any pass on this claim concerning Nicaea. It wasn't appealed to in any of their documents or at their Councils.

Bishop Epiphanius of Salamus in Cyprus (315-403), who became a bishop about 50 years after the Council of Nicaea, declared that the Church admits to the priesthood only those who have renounced their marital relationship or who have become widowers. Priests are chosen, he said, in the first place from celibates, then, if there is a shortage, from widowers and those willing to renounce the use of their marriage.

The African bishops, at the Councils of Carthage, had before them the full text of the canons passed at the Council of Nicaea, and clearly they saw nothing in them contrary to their own tradition, that married men, who became priests, were expected to live as brother and sister with their wives.

The claim concerning Paphnutius and Nicaea was clearly a fabrication composed by those who wished to undermine the rule on the renunciation of one's marriage. The clear evidence is that Nicaea upheld the rule that married men, when ordained, could not continue in their marital relationship.

Conclusion

I have stated that, for research purposes, one could divide the early Church into 5 regions:- Western Europe , Rome and Central Europe, North Africa, Jerusalem, and the East, and that if one discovers that something was being lived and taught in each of those regions with considerable uniformity around the year 350, then one may accept with utmost confidence that this is an authentic apostolic tradition.

In the early Church the rule was the same in Western Europe, in North Africa, in Rome, in Palestine and in the East. Married men could become priests, but once ordained, they were expected to abstain from marital relationships. A single person, once he was ordained a priest or even a deacon, could not marry; nor was a priest free to remarry if his wife died.

This rule could not have been introduced without major controversy, if it didn't come from the practice of the Apostles, and there is no evidence of such controversy. If it goes back to the Apostles, they must have derived it from their understanding of the teaching of Jesus Himself.

Any discussion on celibacy today needs to take full account of this early Church tradition. To allow married men to be ordained but then expect them to live in a brother-sister relationship with their wives, would be in total harmony with the practice and teaching of the early Church. To introduce married priests, with the priest free to live in a full marital relationship, would, on the other hand, be contrary to the teaching and practice of the early church.

Footnote re celibacy in the early Church

For a complete account of the history of the continence rule in the early Church see, "The Apostolic Origins of Priestly Celibacy" by Christian Cochini, Ignatius Press, 1990, originally written in French in 1981 or, "The Case for Clerical Celibacy', by Stickler, Ignatius Press, 1993. Another book has also just been published. It may well be more readable and include new material.

Footnote re Baptism in the first 350 years

Just as I have shown that the rule on separation from one's wife was understood in the same way throughout the early Church, so too one can take Baptism, and show that right throughout the early Church, they had great expectations concerning what would happen at one's Baptism, how one was united with Jesus, how one came under the influence of the Holy Spirit, how one came into Father's love, and how one was expected to live the transformed life.

One could show that this was so in Western Europe, in Rome and Central Europe, in Jerusalem, in North Africa and in the East.

See "Christian Initiation and Baptism in the Holy Spirit - evidence from the First Eight Centuries" by Kilian McDonnell and George T. Montague, The Liturgical Press, 1991.

24

Answering the arguments against celibacy

Arguments based on the falsification of Church history

Argument One
"The Eastern Orthodox Church which is in communion with Rome allows married priests, therefore we should also."

While the rule of married priests living a brother-sister relationship with their wives, was upheld in the East in the early church, eventually abuses crept in. Church leadership was very weak, and there were ongoing divisions and disputes. When priests began to ignore the rule, there was nobody to stop them, and once some were allowed to do it, others followed.

Eventually the rule itself was overturned at the Second Council of Trullo in 691. This council has never been recognised by the Western Church. To justify their approval of priests having full relationships with their wives, the bishops at Trullo falsely claimed that the African Councils at Carthage had permitted such a practice. The Councils of Carthage had permitted nothing of the sort! However few in the East would have been familiar with the Councils of Carthage. Very few would even have been able to read the Latin texts of these Councils. Put bluntly, the Council Fathers at Trullo falsified Church documents to justify the abolition of the rule of separation from one's wife. Thus the abolition of this rule was based on a lie.

We long for Church unity, but above all we long to be totally one with Christ's plan for His Church. This involves honesty both concerning the failures within our own Church and also the failures within other Christian Churches. While the Orthodox Churches have many noble qualities, yet since allowing their clergy to live full marital lives, they have become very poor in evangelism, very poor in missionary zeal, and very poor in the ability to challenge society. What has happened in the Eastern Churches makes a very poor advertisement for a married clergy.

Argument Two
"Many of the early priests were married."

True! However while, in the early Church, married men were ordained, they were expected to live as brother and sister with their wives. And priests were never free to marry after ordination.

Argument Three
"The introduction of the rule of continence only happened when priests began to offer Mass daily."

There is no evidence whatsoever that this was so. All the evidence points to this rule going right back to the Apostles.

Argument Four
"There was the mistaken notion that somehow it would be unseemly to have sexual relations the evening before celebrating Mass."

Those opposing the continence rule in the early Church, argued from the Old Testament practice whereby priests had only to abstain from sexual relations while serving in the Temple. They argued that priests should only have to abstain on days when they offered Mass. Those upholding the continence rule, tried to counter this argument, and hence the debate centred on whether it was right to have sexual relations the night before celebrating Mass. However it was never accepted, that if one knew that one wasn't celebrating Mass, that one could resume marital relations. The rule of continence originated not because of attitudes to sex, but because the priest is called to leave everything to follow Jesus, and called to a special share in the ministry of Christ, the Bridegroom.

Argument Five
"During the middle Ages, there was concern that parish property would be handed on to priests' sons, and this too became a strong element in the prohibition of married clergy."

Problems with inheritance played a role in the change from the rule of continence to one of celibacy.   But inheritance was a problem even when priests were faithful to the rule of separation from their wives - as they already had children prior to ordination.

One could argue from this that the Church could go back to the rule that existed prior to then; that married men could be ordained but would then be expected to live as brother and sister with their wives. It is not logical however to argue from it that priests should be free to marry or to have full marital relationships.

Argument Six
"Priests were free to marry until 1139."

That most certainly was not so.   Prior to 1139 if a priest married, he was to be removed from his ministry, defrocked.   Sometimes when standards were low, this didn't actually happen, but it was still the rule.   However at the Lateran Council of 1139, it was declared that not merely was such a priest to be removed from office, but that furthermore his marriage wasn't even valid.

Other Arguments

Argument Seven
"The law of celibacy is a Church law which can be changed.   It did not come to us from the revelation of God or the command of Jesus."

Yes, the rule of celibacy is a Church law.   However it springs from the radical call of Jesus for disciples who would leave all to follow Him, and also from the priest's special sharing in the priesthood of Jesus, the celibate Bridegroom.

The radical call of Jesus demands a form of separation from family ties.   In the early Church, they responded to this call by allowing married men to be ordained, but then expecting them to live as brother and sister with their wives. Today we live it through the rule of celibacy.   Both are church rules, but they are both based on the radical call of Jesus:- a call that demands separation from those family ties that bind one in an exclusive way, and that invites one to a special share in the priesthood of Jesus who gave Himself totally and completely for His people.

Argument Eight

"People want, need and deserve ordained ministers. It is a scandal that so many parishes no longer have Mass celebrated."

A) Yes this is a scandal but if the will was truly there, suitable candidates for the priesthood could be found. Are there not single people, widowers and even excellent separated people in every area? The rules concerning training for the priesthood urgently need to be revised. They were formulated specifically for the preparation of 18 year olds, to give young men time to mature. There is no reason why a 50 year old should have to go through the same process. But, if those regulations were dealt with, it would be possible for a bishop to go into any parish and say, "Find me a suitable candidate and, after basic training and instruction, and after testing his suitability, I will ordain him."

B) It is very clear that Jesus never lowered his standards by even one iota in order to increase numbers or reach more people. The rich young man was very interested in following Jesus, but he wasn't prepared to let go of his wealth. There is a cost to pay for those who desire Christian ministry, and it is not the will of Jesus that people be accepted who are not prepared to pay the cost. Only those who are willing to undergo some real leaving of family and property can incarnate Jesus in the way demanded for ministry; only they are truly ready to "Do THIS", that is stand before their people and declare, 'I am ready to give my life for you. I desire to live my life for you.'

C) The number one reason for the shortage of vocations today is that the transforming power of the Gospel is being neither lived nor preached. Jesus said,

"You shall receive power when the Holy Spirit comes upon you; and you shall be my witnesses ... to the end of the earth" Acts 1:8.

There is a real lack of Spirit power in the Church today and because of that, we have lost the zeal for witnessing and even the ability to witness. If one truly experiences Jesus as the Bread of Life and begins to live the transformed life, one desires to spread the Good News.

Argument Nine
"Celibacy is responsible for the terrible cases of paedophilia and for all sorts of sexual problems."

Celibacy isn't responsible for either paedophilia or sexual problems. However segregation did play a part; but a much more serious factor is the failure to preach the full Good News of the power of Jesus to transform lives. Expecting people to live the religious life, without leading them into a deep experience of Jesus as the Bread of Life, and without leading them on the path of rebirth from within, is an absolute disaster.

Meanwhile experience in armies shows that, if a heterosexual is cut off from contact with eligible females for a very prolonged period, he may find himself attracted to males. Where a young lad went into boarding school at 13, went straight to seminary afterwards, then back to work in an all male institution, it did create the danger that, if he suffered from sexual compulsions, his desires would focus in a wrong direction. Something similar can happen if a person's shyness causes him to segregate himself.

It is important that a priest have good bonds with female friends. This will ensure, if he is normal, that if he experiences desires or difficulties, it will at least be towards females of his own age. That does not however justify any wrong relationship. Being involved in a wrong relationship is seriously wrong for a priest. He is living a lie; called to give himself for all, and yet giving himself to one.

What is more, the woman experiences hurt in a very deep way. Have you noticed how the mistresses of priests have set up a special association, but the mistresses of politicians and of others have no such association! That speaks for itself.

Yet, although it is totally wrong for a priest to have an affair, sometimes, just like with a married person, a priest may have to work through a phase when he is vulnerable to such relationships. Once again healing and deliverance are possible. Jesus loves such a priest - as He does all sinners. It is His desire to come in a very special way into the priest's life, to become the Bread of Life for him. When that happens, Jesus can then lead the priest on the path of inner transformation. But the priest needs to really seek this transformation and deliverance, and must be willing to take the practical steps necessary, including breaking off the relationship.

There is, however, a grave injustice in expecting priests to be able to live celibacy without enabling them to experience Jesus as the Bread of Life. One needs to have Jesus as one's best Friend. One needs to be actively seeking, and on the way towards, complete rebirth, ongoing personal transformation. Otherwise one will be working out of human power and not Spirit power.

Becoming open to Jesus as the Bread of Life, and becoming open to rebirth and transformation are not optional extras. They are the very heart of the Gospel. A priest absolutely needs them. It is essential that he experiences the life giving water welling up within, essential that Jesus becomes his best Friend, essential that he embraces the need for rebirth, essential that he becomes open to ongoing transformation, and essential that he ends up working out of Spirit power, not human power. Anything less than that is tragic and has the potential to destroy.

Before us there is a crossroads. One road leads to sorrow, to brokenness and to problems; the other to healing, to transformation and to real joy and strength. One road leads to an experience of inner death, the other to wonderful new life. Choose life! Nothing short of it suffices if one is to stand in the place of Jesus.

Argument Ten
"So many priests are involved in relationships that it would be better to drop the celibacy rule."

Dropping the celibacy rule will not transform the heart of any priest. Indeed, in offering a cosier life, it may even prevent him from recognising that his heart does need transformation. What we really need are priests who truly have experienced Jesus as the Bread of Life, who are living the transformed life, and who have been filled with joy by the Holy Spirit. Then living celibacy becomes increasingly easy.

Footnote re quotations
While the ten quoted arguments against celibacy are actual quotations from different people, I am not giving their identities as I do not wish to cause hurt.

25

Growing in the power

*"You shall receive power when the Holy Spirit comes upon you; and
you shall be my witnesses ... to the end of the earth" Acts 1:8.*

I am just a very ordinary person. Neighbours who remember me
growing up will probably remember a young lad who found it
hard to mix, a young lad who was inclined to stick his head in the
TV. Those who remember me from secondary school, may well
remember me as a 'down-and-out' hanging around on the fringes.
Fellow students from Maynooth probably remember me from the
playing pitches, but not for my skill, as much as for a determination
that sprung largely from a need to prove myself. Those who
remember me from my early priesthood may well remember me
as judgemental, sharp, over sensitive and a poor mixer. Those
who know me today will be conscious of my impatience and of
how I get uptight for I still have feet of clay.

Yes, I am a very ordinary person, but I am blessed in coming to
know a most extraordinary God, a God who is very willing to
enter into the life of a sinner like myself and to do a great work of
transformation. My life is a testimony to the fact that even a very
ordinary person, a person who has had serious problems, a person
who continued to stumble and fall for a prolonged period, can yet
reach a truly remarkable level of intimacy with God, can come
into a truly powerful relationship with Jesus, can have his life
transformed, can begin to experience the fruit of the Spirit in a
spectacular way, with joy filling his inner being.

God is like the furniture restorer:- He is prepared to take an old
battered and broken piece, and to work on it until it has been
completely transformed.

The one quality which I have, which has separated me from

many others, is perseverance. I have been prepared to keep going when others have drifted off. I have been prepared to hang in there and to keep searching when others have given up. I have been prepared to keep coming back seeking more when others have rested happy with what they had. I have been willing to go to any person or any place, where people appeared to be walking in the power of the Spirit, so long as what they were doing was consistent with the New Testament and with our Church.

Those who know me today may begin to catch a glimpse of the joy and happiness that fills my life, and the truly wonderful level of intimacy I have with Jesus. Originally I did expect to receive more blessing quicker and easier, yet today I am experiencing far more than I ever thought possible.

At first, I thought that I could become open to the power straight away, that a power would come upon me from on high, and that I could then do spectacular things. It was a bit like the temptations that Jesus endured when He was tempted to do the spectacular, the difference being that He could have done so. Doing spectacular things would have been great for my ego in those early days when I felt so inferior, felt such a need to prove myself.

God's plan, however, is even more spectacular still. He desires to transform us from within. He desires to penetrate us with His love. He is willing to keep working on us until our entire being has been flooded with His light and indeed with His living presence. Then there will indeed be power, an energising power to enable us to have an inner energy, a new strength, a greater capacity to keep going when we are answering His call and carrying out His will.

I attended the 1999 Irish National Charismatic Conference. The chief speaker was a 78 year old, Babsie Bleasdell. She was full of mental and physical energy, the mental and physical stamina of a 50 year old. She is just one of a number of remarkable people who are clearly working out of Spirit energy, Spirit power. Pope John Paul is another. His body is crushed by Parkinson's disease. He can barely walk. Yet his spirit is full of energy and he continues to write, speak and travel at an amazing pace.

Since I got down to doing this book in earnest, I have been

working remarkable hours. I should be very tired, even wrecked and drained. Instead I am full of joy and energy. My eyes get tired from the very long hours looking into the computer, but my spirit feels totally refreshed and renewed.

Father's plan for us is truly spectacular. It is to restore us to what man was like before the Fall; to draw us into a life of breathtaking intimacy with Himself, like what the Bible says Adam and Eve had before they sinned. It is to enable every person to be the hands of Jesus, the voice of Jesus, the love of Jesus in our troubled world, and to experience a deep sense of privilege in being chosen to be partners in God's work.

Before this is possible, tough choices have to be made. Firstly we need to be willing to seek Jesus, and then, when we find Him, we need to be willing to become open to what He offers. This can only happen if we renounce our selfish ways of behaving and learn to do things His way. We must also be willing to persevere in seeking to grow in our relationship with Jesus, and in our openness to the Holy Spirit, so as not to be like the seed that fell on the shallow soil or that grew up amongst the weeds. We must,

"Learn to live and move in the Spirit; then there is no danger of your giving way to the impulses of corrupt nature." Galatians 5:16
(Jerusalem translation)

The work of the Spirit is to help us come into the new life that Jesus offers, to help us to open ourselves to transformation. If we are truly open to the Holy Spirit, we will be transformed from within. Only when this has happened, will we begin to receive the fruit of the Spirit and the power of the Spirit. Only then will our lives be filled with joy and with Spirit energy.

The transformation consists of two elements:- being filled with the love and being penetrated by the light.

Our spirit needs to be filled with love, to be filled by the indwelling Jesus. Many people's spirit are as limp as an empty balloon. Instead of their spirits radiating love, joy, and power, their entire personalities are dominated by their heads and by negative feelings. Then they want someone to give them a blessing to take away the sadness or to remove their worries, when what they really need is to receive Jesus as the Bread of Life, learn to depend on Him and then have their limp spirits filled by the Holy Spirit.

In learning to depend on Jesus, one can find the strength for victorious living, gaining victory over what is pulling one down, with one's spirit being gradually awakened in the process. Then one can progress to having one's spirit truly filled, experiencing several blessings and even healings along the way, as the love of Jesus penetrates new areas of one's inner being.

Being prayed with can, of course, be a real help, being at once a renewal of one's own entrustment to God, and an occasion for anointing. Yet Jesus told the Apostles,

"Receive the Holy Spirit" John 20:22 .

He didn't say a prayer for them to receive the Holy Spirit. He told them to receive the Holy Spirit. For three years He had been preparing them. Now He instructed them to receive. But even then it wasn't immediate. There was yet a further phase while they waited and prayed,

"Behold I send the promise of the Father upon you; but stay in the city, until you are clothed in power from on high" Luke 24:49.

After all the learning and preparation, after being with Jesus through everything, after all they had seen and heard, they still had to seek for something more, they still had to pray and wait. For them, this further waiting was brief, whereas I was like the Israelites in the desert. I wandered in circles, often blocking my own progress, so that it was many years from the time that Jesus touched my life to when I began to really experience the power.

I was indeed already experiencing it in part - like all the times when, as a young priest, I went out to preach depending for strength from on high to be able to face the people. But my spirit was not yet truly flooded nor was I yet penetrated by the light of Jesus. Jesus had truly become the Bread of Life for me. I was experiencing His love in a special way, yet He wasn't even Lord of my then self-seeking spirit, no more than He was Lord of my emotions, or of my memories, or of my sexuality. Until He truly became Lord of my spirit, His love could not radiate into other areas of my being. I didn't even know then that one's spirit could radiate; didn't know that it could actually be inflated by the fruit of the Spirit, by love, joy and peace; didn't know that the power of God present in one's spirit could begin to radiate into and even overshadow one's mind and one's emotions.

In the early Church when the Holy Spirit came upon people, their spirits were so filled that they started to speak in tongues. *"They were all filled with the Holy Spirit and began to speak in other tongues as the Spirit gave them utterance" Acts 2:4.*

We get into such a major knot about whether tongues is a real language that we miss the entire point. It doesn't matter in the least whether tongues is a real language or not. Father knows exactly what is in our spirit and what our spirit is saying.

If the Holy Spirit desires for some person to understand what our spirit is saying then the Holy Spirit can look after it - just as an American priest, Fr. Tim Deeter, went to Medjugorje as a complete sceptic and the first evening listened to Fr. Jozo's sermon in Croatian and understood every word in English. Even at Pentecost, since everybody heard them in their own native tongues, it was a miracle of hearing rather than of speaking.

Tongues is the language of the spirit and expresses what is in the spirit. If one's spirit is bitter, one's speaking in tongues will be bitter. If one's spirit is empty, one's speaking in tongues will be empty, hollow. If one's spirit is pushy or self-seeking, so too will one's speaking in tongues. But if the Holy Spirit is flooding your spirit, then, if you yield to tongues, it too will be Spirit filled.

In speaking in tongues, if one is both truly open to the Holy Spirit and can let go of one's inhibitions, one is giving the Holy Spirit a special opportunity to minister to one's spirit and one is giving one's spirit a chance to soar, to radiate, to develop. It is a truly powerful vehicle for allowing one's spirit to be filled by the Holy Spirit, and so a powerful vehicle for growing in the joy.

As one grows, one's speaking in tongues should become the joy bursting forth. That is what happened at Pentecost. They were so filled with the joy that it had to burst forth. That is the way it still happens for some today. But it wasn't the way it first happened for me. Yet today, for me, tongues is both a natural outlet for the joy and an opportunity to grow further in the joy.

But even if one isn't into tongues, there is still so much that one can experience. Jesus can still fill your inner being and draw you into a relationship of remarkable intimacy.

I have always needed to tease things out, to understand them, to test them, before being willing to yield to them. I was walking with Jesus for 25 years before I began to use tongues with any regularity. I can now see the difference that proper use of it can bring, but equally I had come a truly great distance without using it. Actually it is also possible to 'pray in tongues' in English. I often find my spirit praying without any instruction from the head, my spirit pouring forth a prayer of praise and love. This comes far more naturally to me than the other tongues.

I have been prayed with by all sorts of famous people, but I have never been 'slain in the spirit'. That is the name they use for where a person ends up lying on the floor after being prayed with. I am not frightened of being 'slain in the spirit'. But I do believe that if one is truly 'slain in the spirit' that it should be a life-changing experience, that one should get up converted, changed, healed or delivered. People who fell down when Jesus prayed with them got up healed. When St. Paul was 'slain in the spirit' on the road to Damascus, he got up a very different person. If a person gets up significantly different, then it is God's work. If a person gets up without any real change, it is most likely man's work. Often it is merely a distraction, and results in genuine people being frightened or confused. That is certainly not God's wish.

The main thing, however, is receiving Jesus as the Bread of Life, experiencing the life-giving water welling up within so that one does not thirst again, being enabled to face what needs to be faced in one's own life, learning to entrust every part of one's inner being to the light and love of Jesus, having the Father become one's 'Father', and becoming open to the Holy Spirit so that one can have a real experience of being filled with love, joy and peace. All this can happen without any dramatics, and it is available to anyone, regardless of what has happened in one's life, if one is truly prepared to seek it.

This book does not do justice to my own failures, nor to the extent to which I still have feet of clay, especially my impatience. Neither does it do justice to the level of brokenness that was once in my life. I am writing this section while back in Maynooth for my Silver Jubilee. I have just gone for a walk through the grounds, going to spots that had special meaning for me, going back now filled with great joy and happiness, and embracing the memories of when I was a young student suffering real inner anguish. I stood for a couple of moments beneath a fourth storey window that I once was very tempted to let myself fall out through, my present joy embracing the past pain. That incident, triggered by watching a sad film, was what convinced me to leave the seminary. Thankfully Jesus had a better solution.

God is fair. I am a very ordinary person with feet of clay, but Jesus has led me on a truly remarkable journey. Jesus loves you every bit as much as He loves me. What he did for me, He will be thrilled to do for you.

The question is:- how much do you desire it? Do you really desire to experience Jesus as the Bread of Life? Do you really desire to have your life transformed? Are you prepared to really seek it, prepared to continue to seek and to persevere even when you feel that you are not progressing? Are you prepared to go wherever it takes, in so far as your circumstances permit, to seek what I have found? Are you prepared to truly cry out to Jesus, and to open yourself totally to Him?

If you are prepared to do all this, then have a good talk with Jesus in your own words, asking Him to show you the way.

I often asked Jesus to help me to become as open to Him and to the Holy Spirit as is humanly possible. Nothing ever seemed to happen at the time. There was no rush of power, no special experience, no new capacity to do the spectacular. Yet now I find myself with a relationship with Jesus that is truly fabulous, and an experience of joy that is literally breathtaking. I didn't see my prayer being answered, yet it has been answered beyond my wildest dreams. I can only recommend it to you, first as a decision for you to make, and then as a regular prayer.

Lord Jesus, help me to be as open to You, to the workings of the Holy Spirit and to Father's love, as is humanly possible.

Today my spirit is filled with a sense of love for God, a sense of love that is a beautiful thing to experience. It is lovely to wake up during the night or in the early morning and find one's inner spirit automatically in communion with Jesus, and again to find the same at all sorts of times during the day. Again I see this as an answer to a prayer I have regularly offered for years, the prayer being,

Lord Jesus, I do love you and I desire to love you with all my mind, with all my heart, with all my soul and with all my strength.

Epilogue

Writing this book has stretched me mentally, physically and spiritually. That is a very healthy thing. I have pushed myself, and that builds endurance and perseverance. I have got into the habit of getting up early in the morning. That means that, in future, I will have several extra hours for the service of God's kingdom.

I set out to write a book on celibacy, and ended up writing a book on God's great love; a book for all God's people rather than just for priests. It became, in a very real sense, my own life story; the offering of all that I am to Father and for the service of Father's kingdom as I celebrate the Silver Jubilee of my ordination. That too is an answer to a prayer that I often find my spirit praying,

"Lord Jesus, I offer my whole life to You. All that I am and all that I have, I offer now to You."

I have felt a deep sense of the Lord's guidance while writing. Some insights struck me for the very first time, like how we are invited to call Abba, 'Father', and not 'the Father', just as I would call my mother 'mother' and not 'the mother'.

Footnote for 2001 Reprint

There have been dramatic developments in my life in the two years since I wrote this book, as I feel led into a preaching/ writing ministry. These developments are recounted in my new booklet, "God Has A Plan For You". See page three for details of how to order this booklet and my other publications by post.